More Joy

A
Lovemaking Companion to
The Joy of Sex

EDITED BY
ALEX COMFORT, M.B., Ph.D.
Illustrated by
Charles Raymond
and Christopher Foss

CROWN PUBLISHERS, Inc.
New York

More Joy

A
Lovemaking Companion to
The Joy of Sex

Contents

House Editor: Max Monsarrat
Designer: Janette Place

Editorial Director: Bruce
Marshall

© Mitchell Beazley Publishers
Limited 1973
Illustrations and revisions in text
© Mitchell Beazley Publishers
Limited 1974
All Rights Reserved

Library of Congress Catalog Card
Number: 74-77273
First published in the United States
of America in 1974 by Crown
Publishers Inc., New York

Printed in the Netherlands

Preface

The Joy of Sex, the predecessor of this book, has in one year altered the face of sex education – not in the main by telling people secrets they did not know, but by bringing the healthy discussion of sexuality into what our forbears called the drawing room. It was the first explicitly sexual book for the coffee table.

Its successor covers, as is proper, what *The Joy of Sex* left out – not more techniques or more elaborate ones (there are not many of these), but the two elements of development and of relation. Development matters because, although we make love, or should make it, for pleasure, most people enjoy it more, as they do Beethoven, for the measure of understanding and of consequent growth it gives them. More important, "better" or gourmet sex is a matter not of frantic elaboration – though that can be fun – but of the extraordinary power of this kind of sensuality to transform us, as citizens of an ex-puritan culture, to our good.

As to relation, people no longer uptight about sex itself are in a deep confusion of fantasy, tradition and social change over the expectations to be placed on love, marriage and the like. Much of the fear that used to attend the discovery of sensuality has shifted to the re-examination of fidelity, with religio-social dogmas, personal feelings, fantasy needs, and the deeply proprietorial attitudes to one another enjoined on husband and wife by the priest, the neighbors, folklore and the attorney. The message of the authors is exactly what it was about the physical aspects of sexuality – that there is nothing to be afraid of, and never was, and that we manufacture our own nonsenses.

This is a much more disturbing area, personally and socially, than is the rationalizing of anxieties surrounding physical pleasure. It is possible, though difficult, to have excellent sexual satisfaction at body level without having to run the risks to our defenses inherent in becoming a person. But doing so is a little like using a bicycle solely for stationary exercise. It goes farther with the wheels on the ground. I suspect that what the authors say here about couple relationships and nonpossession – matters which deeply preoccupy all couples even if they have not got round to discussing them – represents roughly what the equivalent of respectable middle-class morality will approve in about ten years' time.

This, then, is part two – if part one was about climbing, this is about mountaineering. The authors have also included a consumer guide to some of the other resources that modern knowledge offers in dealing with problems which you can't handle through reading. Beyond that you are on your own; or rather together – for the main use of this book, as of *The Joy of Sex*, is to read it as the authors wrote it, as a discussing couple.

Alex Comfort

Beyond Advanced Lovemaking

In *The Joy of Sex* we described how to manage the physical side of sex relations. This, like good cookery, is something you can learn, improve and appreciate through learning, and since we have more culture-encouraged anxieties about it than about cooking, books can help by reinforcing our own experience and reassuring us.

On the other hand all sex except masturbation involves at least two people. It doesn't happen at random or in a vacuum, and it is, therefore, about relationship: to have good sex you need a relationship to have it in, whether that relationship is a lifelong partnership or a casual romp between friends. Moreover, all human relationships are sexual, even when they don't look it and don't involve the genitals. We're the only mammal which, probably for reasons connected with our family structure, has used what were originally sexual behaviors as the building-blocks for nearly all our social activities. Some apes use dominance: we use that too, but we sexualize it.

Accordingly, all sexual behavior involves relationship, and most relationship involves sexuality at some point, especially where feelings about our identity, acceptability and so on are concerned. It's not by any means true that sex is the only thing in life, but it is true that getting our sexual identity straight is often the most important way of getting ourselves straight, and that physical sex and the relationships it involves can be the most effective source of self-comprehension if we take the trouble. Half the joy which a couple get from good sex is in their mutual regard and acceptance, and in being actively male or female in a context where there isn't much heart-searching over which is which. Important, too, is finding that fantasy experiences they've always wanted can be shared – and that they work, physically and emotionally. You can feel yourself to be a person in other contexts – landing on the moon, doing a job, winning a match or painting a masterpiece – but sexual identity is a two-way experience. Having had the joy at this level, real lovers will want to take it further; not by devising any new kicks, or even going over old ones to see if they missed any, but by developing the other, relational aspects of sex. They will know by this stage that sexual interchange involves warm feelings of identity and concern, more complicated feelings of dominance and hostility, and tensions between wanting to possess one another and not wanting to be wholly possessed. Rather than be scared by any of these they'll want to understand and experience them.

In *The Joy of Sex* we deliberately stayed off the relational aspect. We assumed that you were either a couple with a relationship who regularly made love together, or that you had some other pattern in which lovemaking took place. To elaborate that and talk about sexuality as a source of personal growth involves going over some of the things we left out.

None of this would probably need saying if we lived in a culture with a fixed pattern, where sexual and social roles weren't open to much choice. If you were a male Plains Indian, you either had to be a warrior, with exorbitant standards of endurance, or dress as a woman to show you wanted out. Men in our culture can be anything from boxers and soldiers (rated very masculine) to dancers and cooks (rated probably gay, though plenty of these are as heterosexual as anyone). Some people aren't worried by this kind of ignorant classification, others are. The same kind of role-prescribing has been used to discriminate against women, who are very rightly in revolt against it.

Parallel with the decline of all this folklore about sexual identity, institutions, like the monogamous one-shot marriage as the norm for all sexual expression, are dying on their feet. People are trying other patterns and have, in fact, more and more choice, economic pressures apart. This choice will grow. Accordingly, either you are half-consciously playing along with one of the prescribed relational patterns, such as marriage, or you are trying to make your own, overcoming a lot of inexplicit learning in the process. You may well decide on a pattern that looks conventional in the end. This book, without talking psychiatry or ethical philosophy, aims to marshal some of the information you need and some of the ideas you should consider in making choices.

Moreover, most of the practical hangups in sex come from not getting your sexual identity and needs straight. Since all of us are biologically and socially male, female, or both at once, most other practical hangups – even the fact of always being put down in business or freaking out when you think you are growing old – have connections with the sense of sexual identity and can be attacked in the same way. There are two sorts of sexual joy – having a full orgasm with a person you value, and being a total person yourself. Since sexual experience is one of the main peak experiences we've left ourselves in this culture, it is on all counts a good place to start, because its built-in reward is love and orgasm. We can't fix this for anyone, but we can and will discuss some of the things involved.

This isn't so much a book about sexual technique: there would be a case for an extended one which would answer questions about how exactly to manage some of the less familiar things, but this would have to be mostly pictures. We're more concerned with the uses of physical sensation and the background into which it fits.

The first section is a discussion of body language. Massage, nonverbal communication, touching and so on have become a California-based cult in which business executives grope each other in hot pools, take bites out of the same sandwich and generally get up steam to have sex when the group leader has finished talking and gone home. If you're already sexually uninhibited it's easy to make fun of this and see it all as sensuality short of being openly sensual, like the poor cat in the adage. On the other hand, sexually uninhibited people underrate the massive block which most folk in our culture have against touching, against physical spontaneity, and against showing affection. This is especially true between males, but almost equally between man and woman, because of our obsession with getting-on-with-it sexually. Some uninhibited people have blockages they don't recognize. Often they are almost totally preoccupied with the genitals – they use the penis and vulva to make love with but not the skin – and they often have surviving hangups, which bob up in unlikely places, about the cleanness and worthiness of perfectly clean bodies.

In view of the size of these hangups, anything which helps people overcome their past miseducation about privacy, separateness, noncontact and so on is a step in the right direction. Others may be more anxious about sex than you and you for your part could probably profit from learning to touch each other, from being touched by strangers of both sexes, and from learning to use your skin and muscles for the sensations they can produce. We aren't going into touching, nonverbalism, massage and the rest as an ideology or a cult, but rather into their uses as a part of the education of lovers.

As a result of our basic cultural miseducation we have three hangups to lose: we have to learn that people aren't dangerous, that the body isn't shameful, and that no rewarding sexual sensation is abnormal or bad unless it's antisocial in some way. It sometimes takes a physical demonstration to change the mind of the child inside us, even if we know these things to be true.

The
Language
of the Body

babies

The best modern sex is nonreproductive. Not only is frequent parenthood now irresponsible, but the development of a recreational erotic life needs privacy. Sexual freedom isn't compatible with a childbearing life-style, and much of what is in this book about sexual equality depends on the pill. At the same time, sexuality is originally reproductive; many people still want and have babies, and the mother-baby relationship is in itself erotic and the genesis of all of the language of bodily contact which figures in adult relationships.

Babies are where adult sexuality starts. They require both the soft texture of the mother and the warmth and probably the odor of her skin, while suckling them can turn her on. Much that is missing in adults has quite probably, on ethological grounds, been lost because we have de-erotized babyhood. People with good erotic lives will put some of that back: by nursing the baby naked; spending at least as much time, in its early weeks, over skin contact as you do in lovemaking; suckling it instead of bottle feeding, if at all possible; letting the baby explore its own body when older; avoiding dirt hangups; and both parents giving continual attention.

All this can be a deeply sensual experience for the mother. At birth, the baby is a little portable mouth and a skin texture not your own which you can carry and apply to your own skin. Normally when it's asleep you will find you put its head on your left breast (women who have had children carry even a parcel this way). The baby is programed to monitor your heartbeat (so that if you get agitated, so does the baby) and be lulled by a rhythmic sound at the normal resting rate.

Generally, the more you handle it the better – when a child is older, pushing its sensual experience can be disturbing, but not at the infant stage: prolonged naked contact is normal for the species. In spite of books you can take it to bed – "overlaying" is another name for what is now called cot death, and not due to lying on the infant in your sleep – but don't make love in front of babies old enough to see clearly. For some reason they read sex as aggression between adults, and there's a poorly understood childhood response to adult sexual odors which is probably better not experimented with until we know more about it. If you put a young baby to breast immediately after an orgasm it'll probably howl, because of your very rapid heart rate. In the first few weeks, all this apart, some couples like to include the baby in gently sensual lovemaking, suckling included – you can even experience having your baby at one breast and your lover at the other (after the baby has finished that side). This can be a most unifying experience. Don't do this later on, but equally don't cut off close skin contact when you can't so specifically include it in lovemaking – just follow the child normally as it becomes a separate individual. Anxiety over naked parental bodies and the father's "dominance" doesn't usually surface under the age of three.

There is an association psychoanalytically in many women's minds between a baby and a penis – both are as it were community property, regardless of the baby's sex. (Male babies, incidentally, get erections early on and nursemaids used to quieten them by bringing on the nearest thing a baby can contrive to orgasm. Some pediatricians now say this overstimulates the child: at a later age it would do, so we can't give an opinion as to whether it's wise or not, but since many primitives masturbate babies it's most likely harmless, and the baby appears to like it.) Don't retract the foreskin on hygienic grounds: it isn't normally capable of retraction until much later, and unless you are Jewish don't cut it off. Penile cancer is a rare hazard; wash, don't amputate.

Women differ about whether birth itself can be a sensual experience; if it's difficult it won't be, nor if the whole setup is clinical. Having the father there is a complicated extra – most men have guilt or co-operation feelings about a woman being in labor which are traditionally taken out as a *couvade* (sham labor for the man) or, in our culture, an attack of toothache or a totally uncharacteristic binge. You'll have to judge if participation will upset him and whether there's an element of demonstration in making him come.

We have no evidence for this, but it wouldn't be surprising if a muscle-relaxed, turned-on and fully orgasm-experiencing woman was more likely to get an easy labor than one who was a bag of tensions. Whether labor can be an orgasm in itself depends very much on luck and on the mother; some natural-childbirth mothers who can relax and haven't been trained by an overrobust nurse say it can. If it isn't, or is painful, that is perfectly easy to control – and putting the baby to breast for the first time is a sensual experience, if only of relief. It's also programed, because breast stimulation makes the uterus contract, which may explain part of the role of breasts in adult lovemaking.

Having a baby, then, is a unique function of your whole body, and a bonding experience with your lover. That's one reason, apart from the child's needs, not to do it solo if you can help it. It's one sexual experience which does commit you, at least until the child grows up.

One has to be careful saying that pregnancy is a beautiful and sensuous experience – a lot of women who have had nausea and felt like a half-loaded oiltanker rightly suspect that this kind of comment is made by males or infertile, butch women. On the other hand most would agree that quickening, one's first encounter with the baby as a person, is pretty moving. Emotional equipment and attitudes also shift in many people while they're carrying – it can be toward anxiety if it's the first time or if the baby wasn't fully wanted, but it can also be toward a gentle sensuality which the man can share. This fits the gentler lovemaking appropriate to pregnancy in all but those women who miscarry easily and repeatedly, and who – this is about the only time it's ever true – do better to avoid orgasms around the time they've miscarried before.

batacas

Soft, cloth-covered plastic-foam bats with which you can box or fence absolutely painlessly and without the least risk of damage. Two people armed with these can belt each other with their full strength without hurting, and women aren't at a disadvantage. The encounter can be merely a fun thing or a dramatization – not, as the makers suggest, of aggression only, but of our far more basic fear that our aggression and other people's would hurt or destroy them or us if it were expressed. This fear goes very deep, and this is a game to get rid of it – it also allows the body language of really violent fighting without any of the bad consequences. Pillow-fights are the nearest thing, but pillow corners can get in eyes and the wretched

things burst if you hit really hard. An all-out bataca fight with someone you love, not hate, can be a very instructive experience in feelings you didn't know you had. If it sounds untender and not the thing for lovers, you probably need it. If she always loses, give her a bataca in each hand against your one, and vice versa. See *Aggression*.

body image

The image we (as observers sitting inside our heads) have of our body. It is much more complex than that, of course, since it's really the whole computer-synthesis of sensory inputs from inside and outside our bodies, plus some added program derived from ideas we have about ourselves in terms of dominance ("feeling seven feet tall," "feeling smaller than a snake's knees") and infant experience. The trouble is that "we" are the computer, so the interaction with our identity isn't that of a controller watching a screen, but far closer.

Most humans manipulate the body in order to manipulate the body image – crowns on kings and bearskins on guardsmen make them "feel big." Obese people who gorge and adolescents who starve are doing the same kind of thing. A whole range of sexual hangups and satisfactions are body-image phenomena, especially fetishes, devices intended to increase or decrease muscle tension, and orgasm, in which the body image momentarily "explodes."

Yogic manipulation runs the other way, and aims to manipulate physiology by manipulating the body image. We now know this is possible (see *Biofeedback*) in quite specific contexts, and nobody would exclude a more general manipulation of things like hormones, fertility, or even susceptibility to disease. This is one reason why self-image is important and goes far deeper than what we see in the mirror.

Yogis, indeed, have several centuries' start on us in investigating this (though with electronic monitors we may catch up). The point of all those odd postures is that they've been worked out to affect body image (originally with the aim of suppressing the body-image component of identity altogether, so that one feels merged with the Whole – orgasm can do the same, whence its use in mysticism). These postures depend on muscle tensions and on crossing-over proprioceptive (from inside the body) inputs – sitting in a crossed-over posture is a little similar in its final effect on body image to the old trick of holding a coin between the backs of two hands – you feel two coins. Some elaborate sexual postures, many uses of compression, restraint of movement, or even tight embracing, and many human semisymbolic interferences with the body, such as corseting or Chinese foot-binding, are basically concerned with manipulating the body image and our experience of it.

The body image is analogous to a telephone exchange and computer store for all the body languages we discuss. A great deal of the medicine and sexology of the future will address the body image as much as the body. What is vaguely described as "feeling more alive," "feeling more a person" after various sorts of experience is really concerned with our own experience of our body as the "computer" scans it. That in turn can alter our body image – and with it our posture, taste in dress, physiology and orgasm capacity. Since body awareness starts at birth and develops rapidly in the weeks when a baby is learning muscle co-ordination, disorders of the body image, often affecting later sexual behavior, probably originate pretty early.

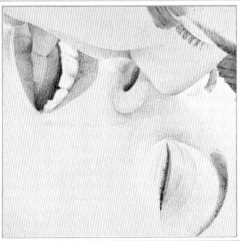

Body Language...
the tenderness and
passion of the act of
love

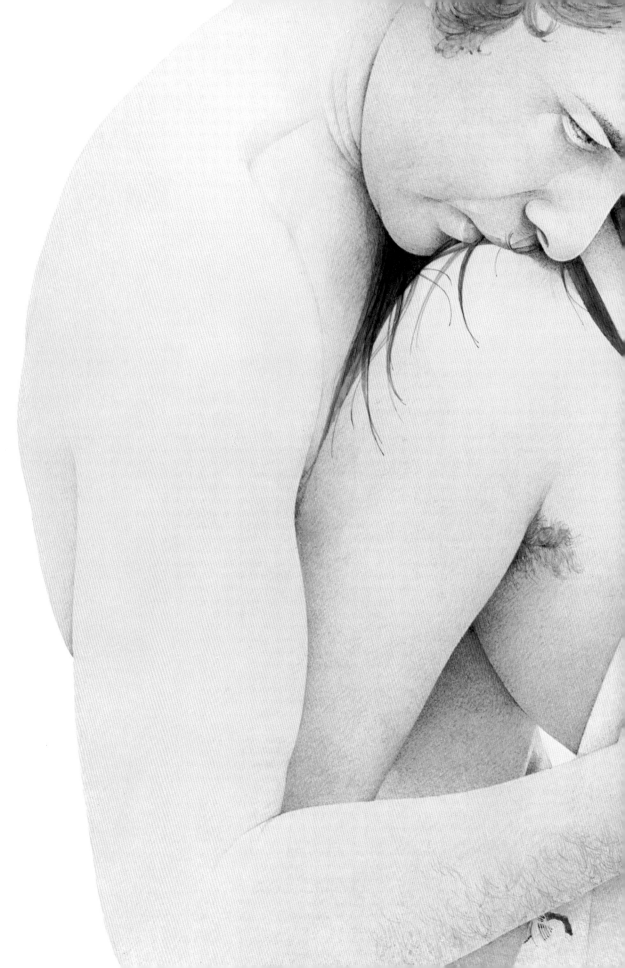

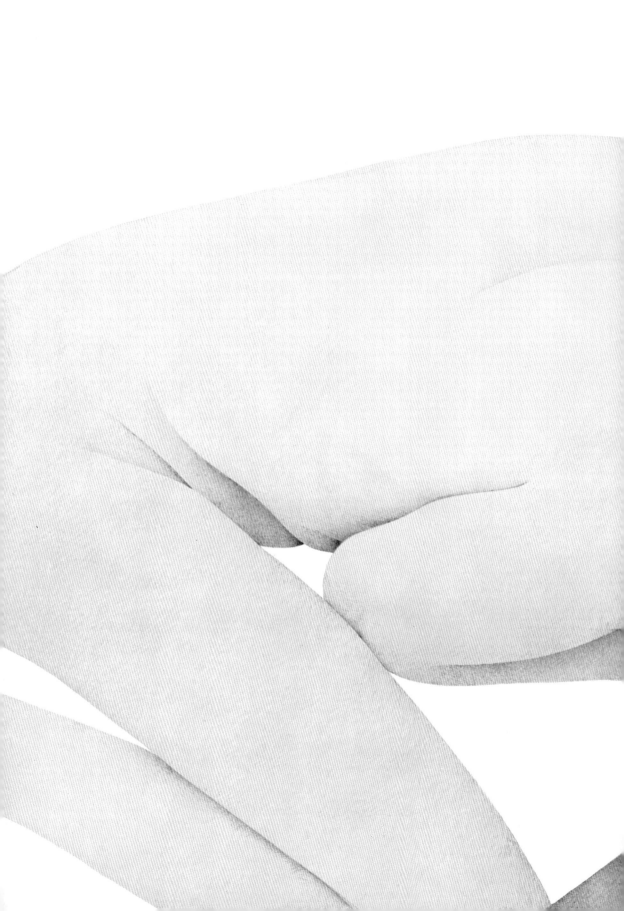

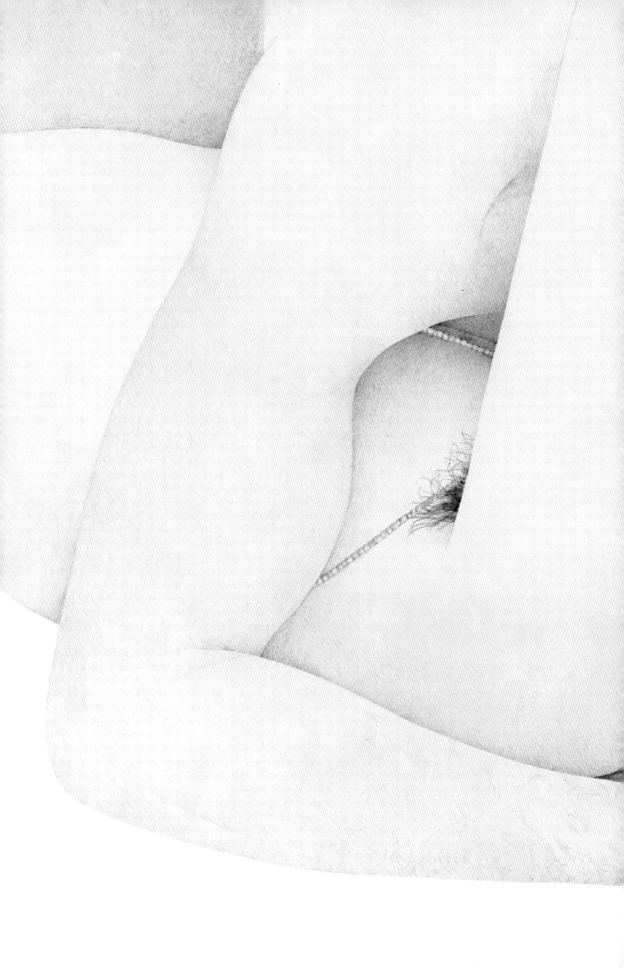

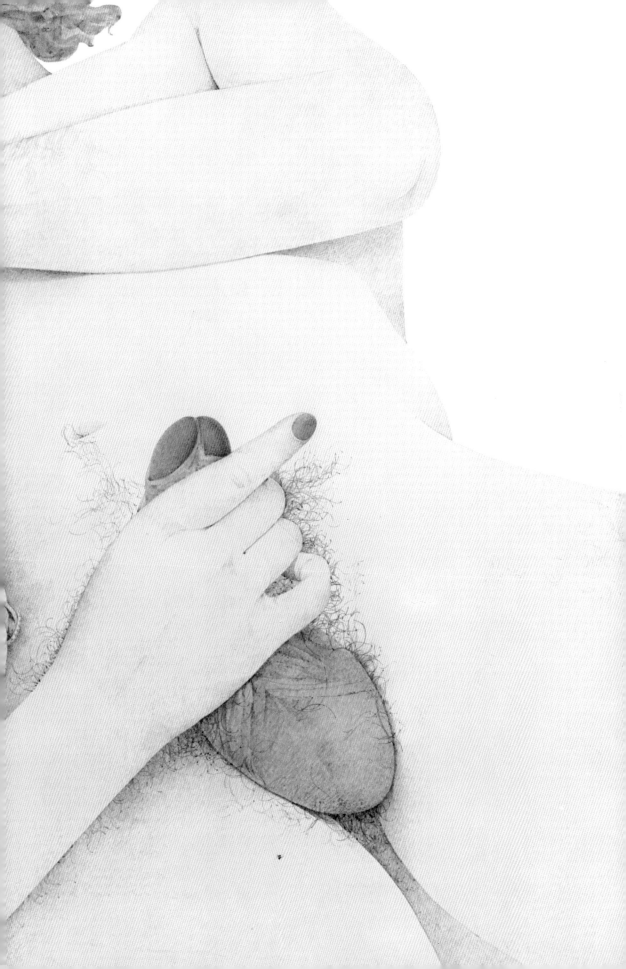

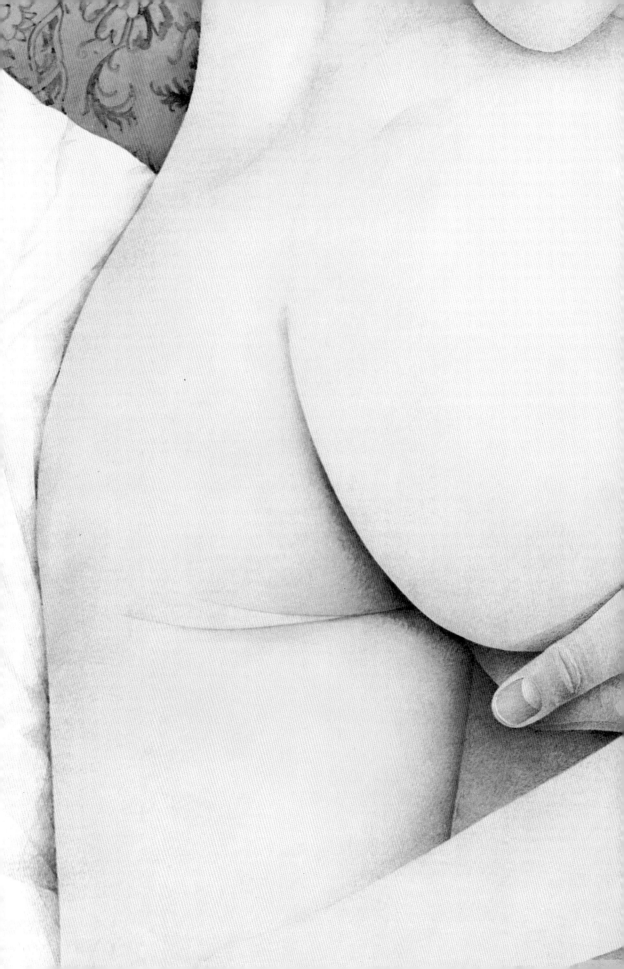

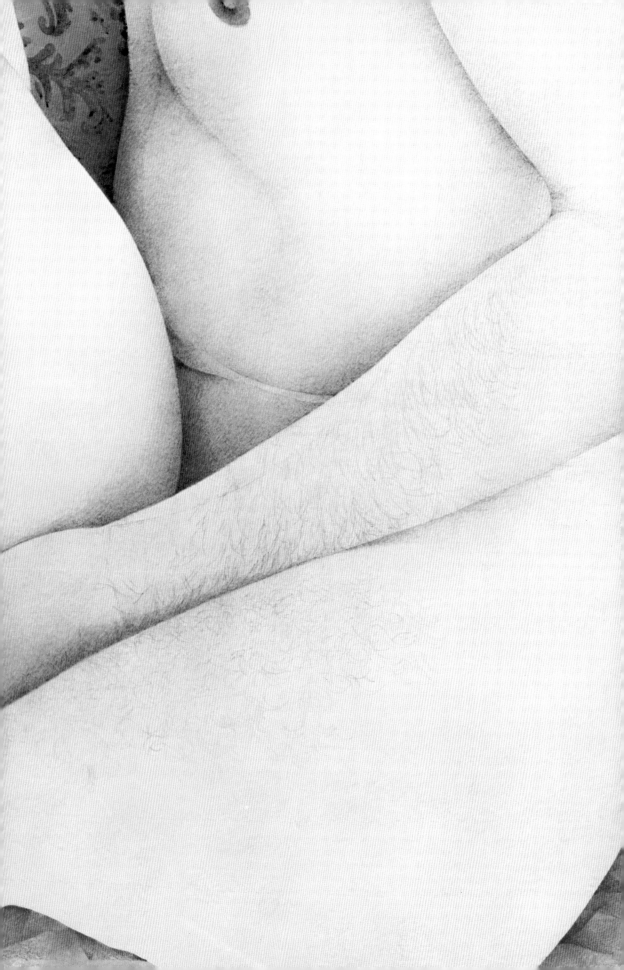

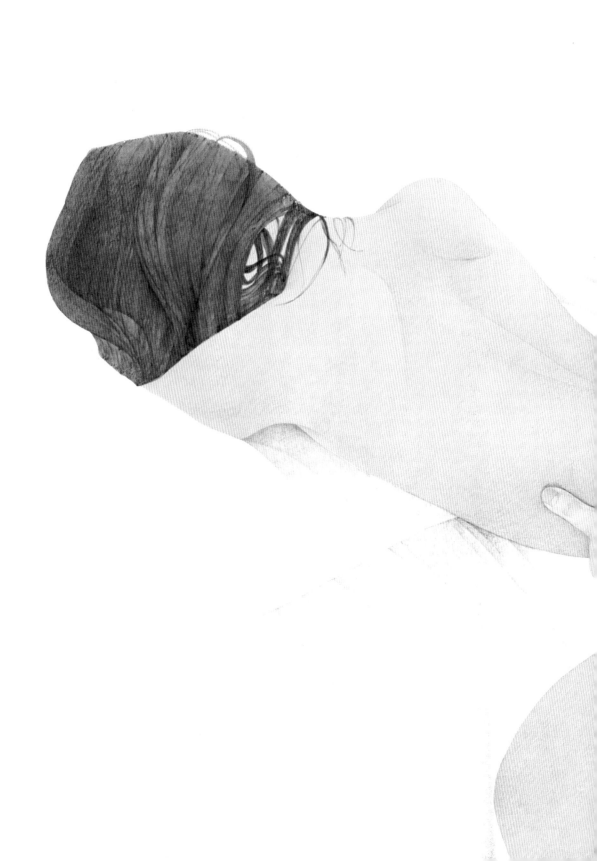

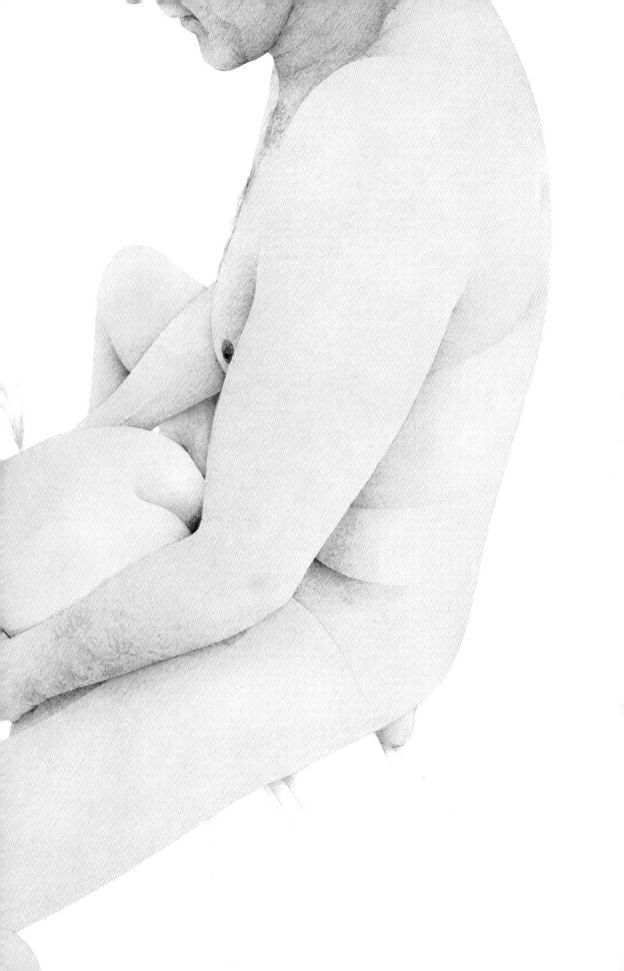

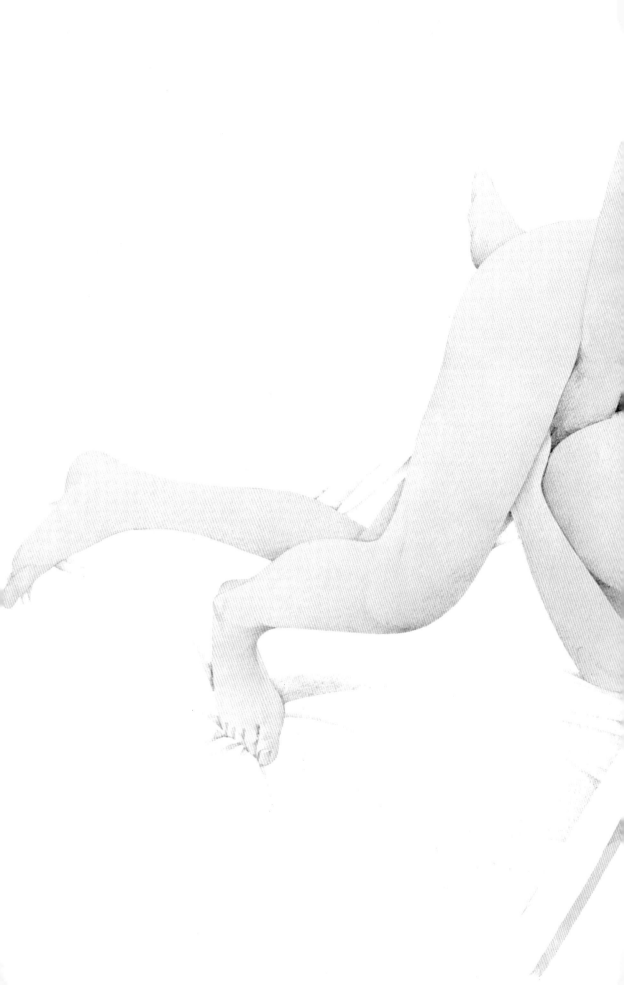

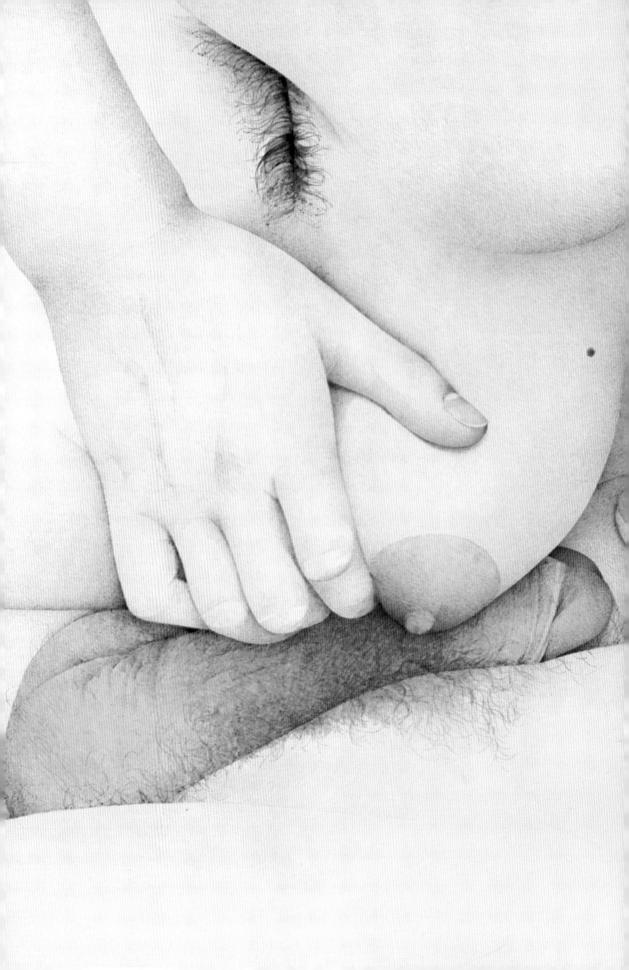

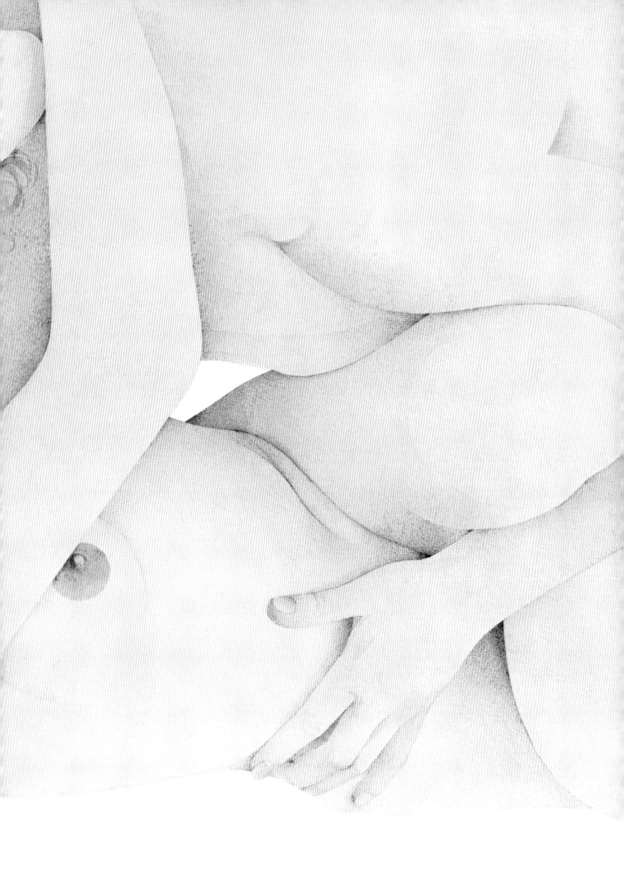

"There are two sorts of sexual joy—having a full orgasm with a person you value, and being a total person yourself"

body language

It was that brilliant eccentric Wilhelm Reich who first pointed out that we use our body as armor against our anxieties. People who feel small and suspicious do hunch up (instead of "walking tall" – the phrase makes the point), and this kind of tenseness generates backache. Other less evident tensions manipulate our body image in other ways and upset our physiology. Moreover, as Reich quite rightly pointed out, the part of ourselves we've been taught to suppress most until recently has been our sexual identity – turning off our skin in case we might feel something sensual, tensing up in case we might have an orgasm, keeping our legs closed. It's a pretty arduous business spending one's whole life keeping one's legs closed.

The phrase "uptight" is absolutely accurate medically. And being uptight nearly always goes back to some kind of anxiety over the expression of normal feelings, many of them sexual. The energy American men have spent trying not to express bisexuality, and American women in not expressing emotions men said they shouldn't have, would solve the power shortage. In uptight people, all of that energy goes into deranging their physiology and turning off their normal human responses.

Accordingly, when we start to live sexually, many of us have to get rid of the batch of cultural habit spasms which prevent us from relaxing and allowing ourselves to feel. It's perfectly good behavioral psychology that if you can persuade the hunched-up self-accuser to stand up, his self-estimate will change and others, who read his body signals, will treat him differently. The same goes for the anorgastic lady who even keeps her mouth closed – teach her to open it and she may feel different.

This is the justification for all the paramedical courses in relaxation, expression and not-being-scared which are proliferating at the moment. Becoming a live body instead of a moralized tailor's dummy can make one act sexually and socially less like a tailor's dummy (and probably cure a lot of uptightness diseases not limited to postural backache). Since half the task of sex education is to get rid of hogwash which people have been taught by disturbed people and have believed, this kind of re-education helps.

Good sex makes us less dummy-like, sickness-prone and liable to destructive pieces of body manipulation, such as compulsive overeating. At the same time, to have good sex, rather than just sex of a sort, we need the total acceptance of our whole body as a source of pleasure, not of guilt, fear, prohibitions, precautions and better-not warnings. In this respect we've still got a fair distance to go as a society. The various sensual things we describe here are intended to move that along.

Animal body language is an important part – since

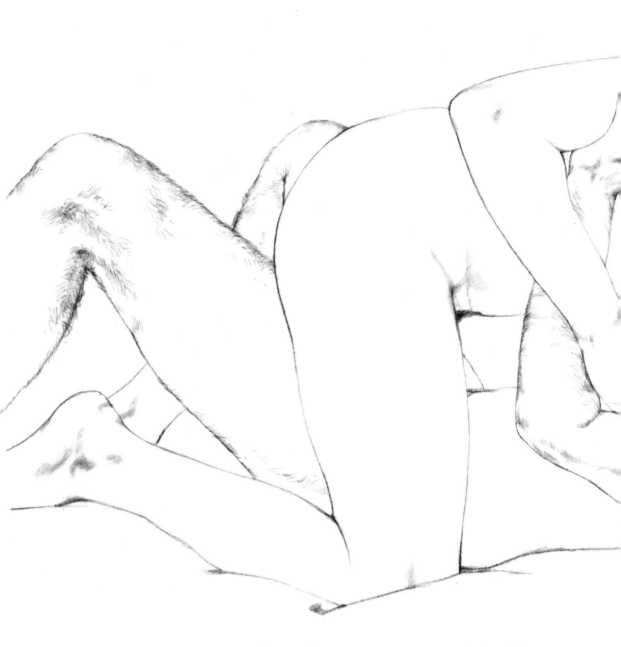

all animal communication is nonverbal – of the science of ethology. Most animals make gestures of self-estimate, which we refer to as dominance and submission. If a male baboon turns his buttocks toward another male and takes the posture of a mating female he's expressing submission, not homosexuality. Baboon society is what is called "agonic," built wholly on dominance and submission, yet this is a gesture which occurs in our own sexual behavior – does it mean the same thing, or some-

thing else, or is it that we have just kept the wiring from our primate ancestors? Chimps are a "hedonic" society: their gestures are invitations to others to behave in a particular way, or statements about how they feel – like being hopping mad. Chimps who give this hopping-mad performance get surrounded by others who are first non-plussed and then supportive or apologetic.

We see this in people, too. The hunched-up person is expressing low self-esteem, and is likely to get pushed

around, which increases his self-deprecation. Body signals which are communicative get reinforced by other folk's reading of them. The tight, mouth-closed lady is saying something nonverbally to men – in this case they are apt to avoid rather than accost her. We all read and speak body language, and more than we realize it can determine our relationships, for it acts at first impression.

hostility

Teenagers today aren't reared on Fred Astaire movies and probably don't get their ideas from *Love Story*. But they do live in a culture where sex equals love. It often does, but it's a lot more complex than that, and even when it does equal love, it can also express hostility. The version in old movies and soap commercials is a simplified version – "lurv" not love – and doesn't occur in real people. It's part of the mythology that loving involves a total takeover bid by each partner for the other ending in a kind of parasitic embrace.

We're not being cynical. If your relation with someone doesn't involve giving, protectiveness and a large measure of sharing it may be a fun thing if both feel the same way, but it doesn't go far as a relationship. At the same time to love or be loved by someone who had no streak of healthy, self-protective selfishness would be a pretty dangerous exercise, leading to unlimited and quite inhuman demand-making on both sides. In fact militant unselfishness is a smart way of making unlimited demands that are hard to combat while at the same time keeping one's end up.

Both sexes need to realize that there is a healthy streak of hostility in all lasting adult love (where it's a defense against being too taken-over by another person) and that some sexual approaches are wholly hostile: notch-cutting by either sex, for example seduce-and-abandon operations by males, husband-hunting by females. Adults can often – but not always – recognize the state of play, but in adolescence one can far more easily get hurt or trapped. In fact in the exploratory relationships common between people who are starting sex, all these components are jumbled up. If they can be expressed as play and seen as play, the attempts teenagers make to see what can be expressed in sexual relations are part of learning. Unfortunately they tend to happen at a time when people are easily hurt. If both are only trying to score, fine – but even here the hostility implied in scoring for its own sake points to a fair amount of inner uncertainty.

Girls have often been already trained by disillusioned mothers to realize that male love can be hostile (and often need to learn that even so it can be concerned and re-

inforcing). Boys don't always recognize predatory behavior by the other sex – and similarly shouldn't be
thrown or scared if they meet it, while not falling for any
kind of blackmail. More important is to look at your own
reading of sexuality to avoid the risk of hurting someone
else. If you think inwardly that all girls or all boys are "sex
objects," are deceitful and need conquering and putting
down, or are basically dangerous, you will hurt someone,
and others who at heart think likewise will hurt you,
unless you are tough to the point of being inhuman.

On the other hand, beginning or practicing sex can't
be wholly painless, any more than beginning or practicing
football. Normal people are robust enough to give a few
rounds to experience. Awareness of reality as against
sentimental fiction helps here, and adolescents shouldn't
be deterred by parents whose own bad experiences make
them distrust and hate all men or all women indiscriminately – a hostility which gets propagated in their
children's attitudes and leads to another unhappy
generation. You will, unless you are lucky, meet hostile
people, be let down, and be sad or disappointed. You can
be prepared for this, as you would be prepared to lose
out occasionally in any other situation: these experiences
only make it easier to avoid settling for the wrong primary
relationship and recognizing the right one when it comes.
You aren't made of glass or jelly, and your final primary
relationship will have a few healthy prickles if both of
you are human.

This book can't stand in for experience, and not all
adults are any more sensible here than teenagers, despite
extra years (which some of them spend reiterating the
same neurotic mistakes). The best response to a letdown
or a putdown if you're young is to cry or swear for not
more than 12 hours, wallow in self-pity for not more than
three days, then write it off to experience and realize you
are that much maturer.

hot tubs

It's been said that it's immoral to take a bath alone. The
communal kind is a Japanese invention. You wash before
you get in, then all soak together. In Japan this isn't an
erotic exploit any more than a sauna, but for us it makes
a remarkably effective icebreaker and a kind of bonding.
People who soak together behave as if they'd shared a
warm womb.

European houses aren't geared to this – they could
be, since the climate in Japan is not so different. Rich
Californians sport a hot Jacuzzi pool; less rich ones buy
up old winevats or construct their own outdoor tubs,
fed by a small waterheater. (See *Hot Tubs* by Leon Elder,
Capra Press, for practical details.) Apart from being the

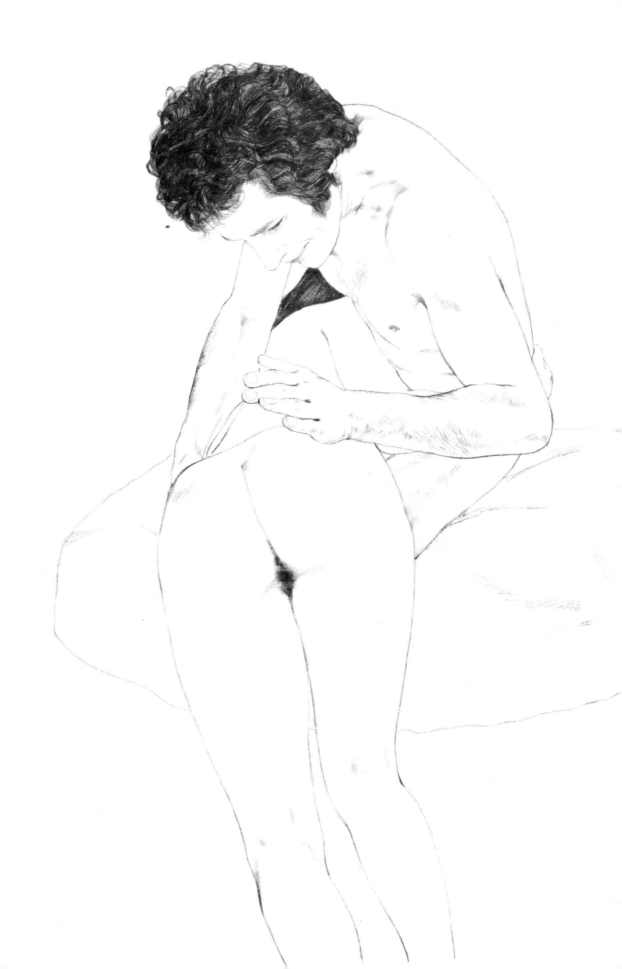

best invention for companionate relaxation since the days of the Roman Empire, hot tubbing encourages non-nudists to share nakedness more easily than swimming. Mickey Mouse hasn't so far persuaded us to wear swimsuits in our baths, so hot tubbing makes a good starter. The tub needs to be around 100°F – it's a site for togetherness and things like group massage rather than lovemaking, for which it's really too hot if you want to be strenuous. We put it in here because it is part of the repertoire of greater sensuality, between couples and between friends, which goes in turn with better sexual expression, and it's a fine start for sharing (q.v.). Ordinary baths and even millionaire "conversation" baths have none of this social quality. The whole thing need not cost more than $250 plus fuel, though it would be costly to keep running – less so in a warm country. Couples who are close enough to make real use of them could own one jointly.

language of the heart

Nothing to do with pink bows and Franz Lehár. The probable reason that the heart is a traditional seat of the emotions is that its rate changes with arousal. This is only readable on close contact or for one's own heartbeat, but the mother's heart rate is a programed signal of her emotional state to a baby at breast (see *Babies*). Between partners their own heart rate and that of the partner act as arousal signals – this, plus infant reminiscences, may explain why heart-like drumbeats in music are erotic (the theme of fate in *Carmen*, the bass in Roberta Flack's "The First Time Ever").

Most lovers do genuinely aim at heart-to-heart contact, often in the infant, head-on-breast situation, so the quickening heart rate is arousing during the runup to sex and the slowdown is tranquilizing during detumescence.

Heart rates in both sexes at orgasm can go as high as in athletics, both from arousal and exertion. Even for people with heart problems such as angina or arrhythmia, however, this seems to be the least hazardous form of exercise – compared with unaroused stairclimbing it rarely produces either anginal pain or extrasystoles, presumably because the coronaries dilate in anticipation. Bed deaths are much more often due to anxiety, it seems, than actual physical exertion, because they don't usually occur in the familiar marital context – much more often during what used to be called an "intrigue."

massage

This isn't a textbook of physiotherapy, so we aren't going into the medical, nor the Oriental, sensual, erotic and other kinds now canvassed. If you want to make a big deal of it you can buy books on sensual massage which come in a kit complete with a bottle of baby oil. Do learn the art of sensual massage, however. It happens to be one of the best presexual turnons for both sexes, one of the best postcoital relaxations, and certainly the best icebreaker. We've seen couples who are really good at it – both of them – get another couple to strip with a decent social excuse and turn them on without being irreversibly seductive if the scene doesn't take off (they can always say thank you and get dressed if that's how they feel). See *Sharing*.

If you've got experience in medical massage, fine. If not, don't just rub the skin, which isn't soothing, but work on a limb or along the trunk with both hands together, kneading fairly firmly but not heavy-handedly with the thumb and fingers. If you do this regularly to each other you'll learn what soothes and what irritates. Try and get a massage from someone good, to see how it feels, and watch them (but don't try professional tricks such as those involving knee pressures on the back until you know how). Don't "rolf" people – this hurts, has no medical basis, and is best left to masochists. Don't use too much oil unless you happen to like the feel of it (you don't need oil for good massage), and when things get really erotic, don't automatically put it on the penis even if massage parlor girls do – it cuts sensation below triggerpoint in some males, though others enjoy it, especially if you're going to massage the glans itself.

You need to be naked yourself, so you can use your whole body surface. In the early stages you can vary

kneading with tapotage (very light, quick karate-chops given with the edges of the two hands alternately and close together on back, thigh and other muscles – do it as if you were chopping onions with two choppers). With the subject face-down put each of your hands on one of their hands, fingers spread, run them simultaneously down each arm, then side by side down the trunk, over each buttock, and down each leg to the foot, with firm finger-pressure. Later on, do the same with the subject face-up, going lightly over the breasts if it's a woman, then down the insides of the thighs. You can add touches from your breasts, genitals and pubic hair if you wish. Not all the most sensual effects come from the obvious areas – careful finger work between the fingers, between the toes, and on the palms and soles (without tickling) can excite most people. Take time to learn what works on each other before you try on someone else – then both of you work on a third party, one giving general massage while the other (usually the other-sex partner) concentrates on special areas such as hands and feet.

Both start together with straight body work, however, and only increase the sensuality if the subject seems to be responding – go on to fingers, armpits, breasts (don't neglect the breast and nipple area in males), insides of thighs with your fingernails (gently) in both sexes, while the same-sex partner keeps up straight muscle kneading. Finally, take a finger or toe in your mouth – if that works, you can begin tongue work elsewhere, ears, trunk skin, nipples. Don't rub the clitoris unless she is manifestly ready for it, but do brush her lips with your nipples or glans, according to how you're placed. When a man gets a full erection you can fondle the scrotum first, then go on either to full masturbation, or if you want to keep with the massage bit and make this something special, oil the glans and rub it between your thumb and finger. The point of sexual no-return is really when you start mouth and tongue work – before that it's sensual massage, afterward it's pre-sex.

Even if it doesn't get that far, being massaged by more than one person is a special sensation: tribal massage by many people, eyes closed, is an experience of deep reassurance rather than a kick. Being massaged, eyes closed, by another naked person using their whole oiled body on your body is a wilder experience. With two couples it's often best for three to work on one person before changing to one-to-one: in a threesome, change roles, or all three massage each other. Don't in either case hurry to switch to full sex, but prolong the oral part, with kissing and tongue massage. For women, when the touching gets specifically genital, the tongue is usually better than the finger. A shy person often takes better to sexual massage if blindfolded (and you may be less blocked about same-sex contacts if the subject doesn't know who is doing what). In fact, in massaging a woman, it often isn't the man who starts mouth work – or who takes it to orgasm.

Apart from its social uses, cultivate prolonged massage of each other, as a couple (oddly enough blindfolding or shutting the eyes often helps here too, even though you know perfectly well who's doing it). Don't forget the head, hair and scalp, or forget that the penis and vulva as well as the hands and mouth are skin-stimulating tools, the vulva in particular because of its warmth. So are all hair tufts, if you're agile, and your head hair and beard if you've got one.

The only problem is that it takes naturally unclumsy and sensual people to give good sexual massage. But you can better this by learning not to grab, bruise or irritate – and in so doing you'll get much better at sex generally.

Group massage, or massage between more than two people, is now a widespread feature of "new encounter" experiences. It does not have to become what society would consider sexual, but equally it can do so. The choice is yours – it is still a good experience if it stops short of genital stimulation and is spoiled by over-concentration on that.

When massage gets really sexual, especially in a three-some, the passive partner usually won't stay passive, or, if they do, they can be invited in – they too have hands and a mouth. When you want to do this, place one of their hands wherever you want it – on a skin surface if you don't want to accelerate the tempo too much, on a breast, penis or vulva if you do – and give them something to work on orally, either a thumb, or something more interesting. If you do this, they will usually stay semi-passive: if you don't, all three of you will probably start to embrace. In fact, if you or they don't want sex this can make a natural endpoint without any letdown, the embrace signifying that it's social not sexual.

If you go on from there, one active partner and the former subject can begin, though not quite at the beginning, with the other. If two women massage one man they often get so involved with each other that he has to wait, but it's worth letting this take its course. Occasionally a threesome massage turns into what looks like rape but isn't (if the massaged party is very turned on, struggles wildly, but clearly wants to continue). Make sure they really do want to continue – massage mustn't become an excuse for sex which someone has reservations about.

Oddly enough, even among those that take it all the way, a threesome developing at the deliberately slow tempo set by massage doesn't usually end in straight intercourse, partly because there's an odd man or

woman out. With two women and one man it much more commonly, and satisfactorily, ends in three-way oral sex; with two men and a woman it's more apt to end with her taking one of them orally and the other vaginally, if she was the one massaged. If she was part of the massage team, she takes the subject while her partner drops out or fondles her breasts: it's difficult for her to give good hand work, except to maintain his erection, while she's getting into orgasm astride, and they may want to turn over at any moment. With two couples, if massage goes on to sex, there's no numerical problem – and also less mutuality. Sexual massage in a threesome can be a very unifying experience, whether it goes on to full sex or not, so don't do it with the wrong person (see *Threesomes*).

Probably the thing most experienced couples most often miss is that the buttocks and small of the back are highly erogenous areas. You can perfectly well turn someone on face-down by the right kind of touches, kneading, gentle slaps and so on. Practice this – from behind you can get at the neck, whole back area, buttocks, small of the back (which is an erection trigger area in males if you find the spot for finger pressure), soft insides of thighs and much of the woman's perineum. Remember you don't have to use massage only before intercourse – you can use it in intercourse (of her back in a rear-entry position, if you have good control, for example). Once she has started on the penis, however, massage of the back, etc., is apt to be swamped by local feeling or to act as a distraction – he may then prefer to concentrate on genital sensation.

How far you take massage depends on whom and where you are massaging. But it's the gentlest form, not of seduction, but of introduction. It's also an excellent way to learn to use and accept your body and other people's.

masturbation and learning

This is now a more important learning experience for the woman than for the man, because quite a few girls don't embark on it spontaneously. Men almost universally masturbate for enjoyment from early adolescence on – they may also use it to desensitize themselves and avoid overrapid response in intercourse: the second of these has to be learned, but not the first. Women who do not climax or who are frigid in intercourse almost always have to be taught in the first instance how to produce an orgasm themselves, before learning to transfer that ability to the sexual situation. This strongly suggests that while boys need only be told to enjoy masturbation without guilt, adolescent girls should be actively encouraged to explore their own bodies. The idea that this is a beautiful love-secret to be taught them only by an idealized betrothed falls down on the inexperience and anxiety of a lot of the unidealized men they'll meet. If they don't know their own responses they can't help a man to stimulate them. The idea that learning in this way will cause them to get stuck with noncoital responses is a piece of theoretical folklore. Shy and anxious people of either sex can get stuck with masturbation because it's nonrelational, but that is as a consequence of their original withdrawnness.

To the mother who finds her daughter masturbating and wants to know what to tell her, the answer is, rejoice and be exceeding glad that she's learning a skill, and hope that if you were worried by old superstitions you didn't show it and put her off. As to "telling" her, say it's something she'll be able to enjoy all her life, a practice for adult lovemaking, and the only way to learn her own responses; warn her against disturbed people who say it's sinful or harmful. Don't give her a vibrator – some adults find that effective, but it's inclined to damp down sensitivity with prolonged use, and is better kept for people already sexually active. If your daughter doesn't masturbate, there would be a case for teaching her if parental teaching wasn't apt to be mistimed and intrusive: books, or instruction in a group as a part of normal sex education, would be a better idea.

Lovers should not only masturbate each other, but watch each other masturbate – both for excitement and instruction. Few women respond best to finger insertion which men tend to use with the idea of simulating intercourse. If your man watches how you do it, he can vary that for new sensations.

One of the most useful things any sexually experienced adult can do is to re-evaluate masturbation. When we start it as kids we don't have the experience to do this, and most of us stay with the technique we learned then and use it as an occasional. As an adult you can go back over this – it's something you enjoy and accept and you now have the privacy to do it properly. If you never saw yourself masturbate, use a mirror, settling down to it naked and in the most comfortable posture. A male should consciously look for new techniques: try with your left hand if you normally use the right (you'll be surprised at the difference), use the foreskin if you normally retract it – if you're circumcised, try wetting or oiling the glans and rubbing only that. A woman should similarly try things she hasn't normally tried – the clitoris alone, if you use the whole-hand method, and vice versa. The object is both to enjoy and to learn more about the responses of which you are capable. If any other part of you seems to need attention, notice. If you have a fantasy, notice that. Then try the same things with your partner watching. He or she will learn new things too.

muscles

Muscle contraction occurs all over the body in orgasm, especially in males, some getting what looks like a convulsion. Involving the whole musculature in the act of ejaculation is about the nearest men normally get to the whole-body sensations women experience in orgasm, though theirs is of a different kind. Most men get a partial experience of this through exertion in intercourse – a passive or totally relaxed orgasm is quite possible for men, but obviously it doesn't make use of this particular body language.

It is, indeed, a language, and this has given rise to some hangups which aren't for once culture-created, but may be basically human. The language of skin contact has been tabooed in our culture because it expresses tender sensuality. Muscular language is for some people even more anxious because it's associated with aggression or violence.

The biology of this is interesting. The male is programed to use a lot of muscular strength in intercourse, and needs to do so to achieve one variety of total-body orgasm. On the other hand a strong individual who really went for this would give his partner problems and might have to hold back, in order to stay on the bed and not bruise her through muscle-spasm. Even with not-so-muscular couples, children who see or hear intercourse are apt to mistake it for a violent assault. This could be behind the notion among social evolutionists that the male of our primate ancestors was programed for struggle because he had to catch and overpower the female (the old caveman joke), and that this tended to promote the survival of the fittest. The explanation's neat, but it only reflects human anxieties, not primate behavior. No ape overpowers the female (who can bite very effectively, and outthreaten a male), and it is normally she who does the inviting – rape is entirely a human invention.

Why we erotize intense muscular contraction in orgasm and then associate it with aggressiveness isn't clear, though it could have something to do with early infant experiences of sensuality and frustration at a time when our musculature isn't very co-ordinated and everyone else is stronger than we are. It may surface preferentially in males because they have bigger muscles and a special hormone system to maintain them: it would be interesting to see if the woman athletes who use anabolic pills to boost their musculature get the same reaction.

At the practical level, some people manage to express this response fully by using positions in intercourse which give them maximum muscular scope. Extracoital things like sport or actual struggle can set off sexual excitement – quite commonly, in both sexes, by watching, not participating. Watchers tend to play over at brain-level the movements they are seeing, so it could be that at least half of the arousal comes from what are really abortive or unrealized movements, though the element of nonverbal communication and symbolism helps. This may explain why "violence" is exciting – an unfortunate association for Man. Another effect of the exertion-equals-aggression equation may be that we could make good use of sexual energy in the interests of civilized behavior. In our culture we're more or less obliged to block the movements that express hostility to people like political crooks, fellow drivers and the guys at work, and lack nonhostile aggressive activities like hunting, running and heaving logs. Apes, on the other hand, make intensive movements and throw things about to express frustration – if we did, we'd be laughed at.

Accordingly, although the muscle-anger equation causes trouble, especially when it's tacked on to mutual anxieties between the sexes about who is stronger than whom, learning to use the sexual language of muscles is a resource, and it can be highly reinforced by the intensity of the climax it gives. Psychiatric writers who see violent physical activity in intercourse as covert sadism are confusing activity with hostility. Real sadism – self-assertion through hurting or humiliating someone – is almost certainly a part of this normal association-sequence gone badly wrong.

Some people need to use other techniques, partly because of the symbolisms which muscular language generates for them. Actual struggle, if it's under control, turns many men on (see *Wrestling*), and it may be because abortive movements are effective and reminiscent of infant sensuality experiences that they often wish the woman were the stronger. Bondage (i.e. binding someone so that muscular tension is maximal but they can't move or get loose) is another traditional method, and the only one which maintains the tension right up to and through actual orgasm: you can't have sex while wrestling. Skillfully done it can give a man an orgasm in which nearly every muscle of the body takes part, making him, in one informant's words, "feel like one huge penis" – a psychoanalytic bonus which probably contributes to its popularity.

This only applies to some of the complicated postures which give tight elbow compression. Couples who nominally tie each other as a preliminary to teasing are mainly acting out a weaker-stronger game (see *Aggression*), and women who enjoy being bound usually also like the dramatization of helplessness. This is another case of a sexual technique which can be played for symbolism, physical effects, or (usually) both. At the physical level a really expert woman can induce an all-muscle orgasm in a man if she secures him correctly, and the muscle response is stronger than in straight intercourse, however violent, because the movements are abortive or isometric, and he can use his full strength. It's been suggested that this explains what Delilah was doing to Samson. Observe, after what we've said, that both wrestling and bondage as sexual extras terrify (or fascinate) some anxious people as violent, aggressive or sadistic. They've got far more to do with body image.

At the other extreme, total muscle relaxation is sexual (in both sexes) and doesn't have any symbolisms alarming to Man because it's a statement of total non-aggression. All the same it can produce all-body orgasm in males who learn the knack, though more rarely than tension because it's not a positive effort and isn't boostable artificially. Really good massage can induce it. It's noticeable (see *Massage*) that the sexual contacts which follow prolonged massage are intense but often, to the observer, rather inactive if it's been properly done. Even work on the penis or clitoris remains massage not masturbation, since the muscular key is lower. For although the feeling is as intense it's different and, with good preparation, more generalized. For the male this is much nearer to the real female pattern, and should be experienced if possible. (It could be that the male orgasm isn't as generalized as the woman's, not only because men

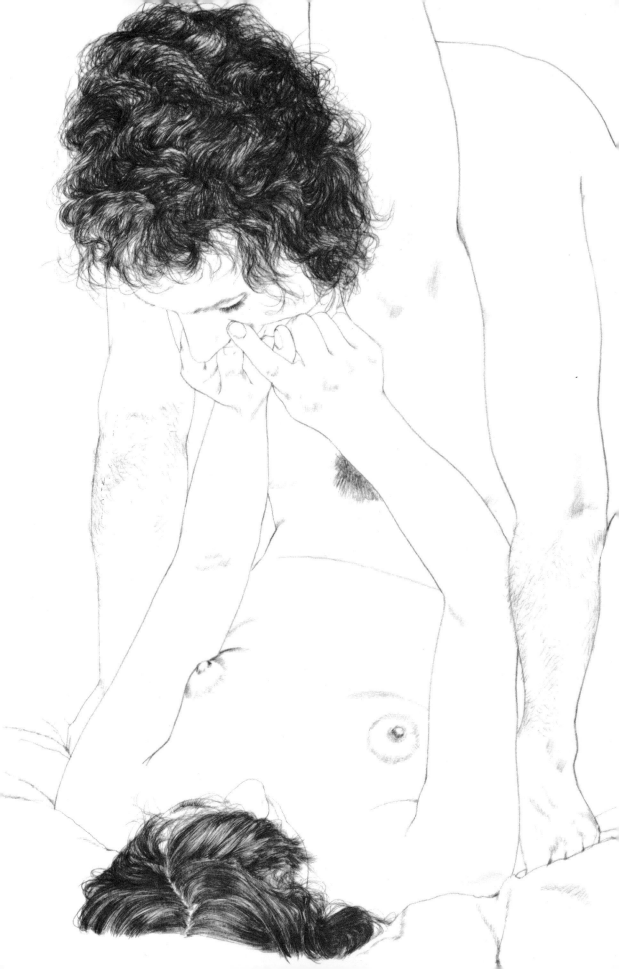

concentrate on the penis, but because they concentrate on their muscles.)

Women, too, use their musculature in intercourse and orgasm, but it's mostly the pelvic and thigh muscles, though it may spread to the back. They have the option of cultivating this (especially the internal pelvic movements, which can be learned) and sharing a male-type muscular orgasm if they want to.

Contrary to folklore huge muscles in the male are not a common feminine turnon, any more than huge genitalia. Muscles, like genitalia, are probably a male dominance signal, which explains the cult of body-building that occupies most of some people's time. The "140-pound weakling" in those body-building ads, who gets hassled by a bully on the beach, takes the course, and then beats hell out of the bully, has some biological basis in male thinking. In the ad, his newly acquired aggressiveness enchants his formerly disappointed girl friend: this is a male fantasy, however, since with most women success in a brawl doesn't rate very high. The only muscular structures that are an important releaser for women appear to be male buttocks.

In gay sex between males, both muscularity and genital size are turnons, because here it is precisely the male dominance signals which are being erotized.

pictures

Sexual pictures are a turnon in their own right (which is one reason we've included them here) and can be uniquely beautiful (which is another). With instant cameras removing the need to get film developed, people are coming to use snapshots sexually as they've so far used them in other family contexts – as a memory file to relive good times – and for this they are extremely effective. Moreover you can use them dream-fashion and realize your own fantasies visually for keeps.

It's unfortunate that only expensive instant cameras can be set for time-lapse, and good pictures of an engrossing activity like lovemaking really need a photographer. We don't ask footballers to photograph themselves. Accordingly, photography goes best in a two-couple scene.

There are a few rules. Don't send sexual film to commercial photographers, especially across state lines. Some will refuse it, destroy it, or send it to the police (and since most of us are breaking obscure sexual laws at every session this could be heavy – the courts really apply these idiocies, and you could be declared sex felons simply for giving each other head): those that don't, and print without a murmur, are commonly taking copies for sale. Unless you want to shoot movies, use a Land camera. If you want motion, save up and get videotape. Keep an album by all means, but don't show other people's pictures around without their consent, as some swingers do. Tact, and an awareness of just how mean and dangerous square authority is when set in motion, are essentials for survival if you have a full and joyful sex life, and doubly so the more people it involves.

You can of course buy sexual pictures as a turnon, but few professionals are as skillful as you could be yourselves. The best use of transparencies is to photograph flowers, lace and textures like striped Indian blankets or rows of eggs in a box, project them and walk together into the beam until it focuses on your skin. Then dance, or make love, watching yourselves in a mirror. It's less messy than body-painting, more versatile, and taps a human turnon we've nearly forgotten – a painted person is magical. If you can get good sexual films you can show them as *hors d'oeuvre*, but this isn't usually necessary when you can do instead of watching – except when you need to turn another couple on.

Keep sexual snapshots and color slides out of the general box you show socially. You'd be amazed how often, if you don't, one surfaces on an inappropriate occasion. Keep your Land camera loaded, focused and ready, particularly in two-couple settings, so that someone can lean over and have it ready to capture anything specially beautiful, or funny, or original. Censor and distribute the prints together before you split up, and make sure the negatives don't go into the garbage if you mind other folk seeing them.

Tapes are an even better turnon – keep the best occasions and play them as background: women in particular are often wildly excited by the right reminiscence.

positions

We didn't elaborate much on these in *The Joy of Sex* because they have been an obsession of sex books throughout history. Experienced couples usually use quite a number of them, but find out by trial and error which produce good sensations and stay with those. They are, however, a part of body language in sex, and not all the experience involved in them is simply a result of a good genital fit.

The missionary position is deservedly popular: it's excellent physically, adaptable, and dramatizes intimacy. On the other hand it is intimacy with the man as the stronger or on-top party. She may feel more or differently turned on if she plays stronger (and on top she actually is stronger, in having more control). Some people see sex from behind as animal – according to them it's bad not

"Splitting the reed" in Indian erotology – a muscle position in which, as well as applying clitoral pressure, he is using his effort to tense her muscles by thrusting on the raised leg. From here she can easily roll over without disturbing the flow into the cuissade (half rear entry) or croupade (full rear entry) positions

to look into your partner's eyes (which most people shut as orgasm approaches anyway). But being taken from behind may be like being taken blindfold: you can't see the man, it makes him a stranger, and that can be exciting; it also gives stimulation of the whole perineum. One can find it rewarding for either or both reasons. Turning the buttocks is also a primate gesture of invitation and/or submission, and that may come into the turnon too.

Quite apart from the meaning and physical efficacy of different postures for people of different shapes, good lovers sometimes try them as a sequence like dancing, not for quick orgasm or regular lovemaking but for variety. Through them they can savor the different physical emphases and the different plays which are dramatized – lover-stranger, weaker-stronger, taker-taking – as a continuous experience, in which all their skin, muscle and genital responses are explored.

Preferred position is part of body language, but don't

play it back idiotically and assume, for example, that a woman who comes on top is naturally bossy. It could be the reverse, as with many games, or she may simply find she gets better physical control that way. Equally, a man who wants it from behind is not necessarily wishing he were balling another man, or undervaluing women. He may simply find that buttocks against his lower abdomen boost his response, or like it deep and half-upright. This sort of anxiety based on the real language of intercourse shouldn't be allowed to replace the older theological anxieties it supersedes. Play it the way you enjoy it, and test your further responses by occasional sessions devoted simply to variety – a language is no good unless you speak it constantly, and the psychological overtones are sources simply of extra stimulation.

It's been remarked that describing sexual positions is a bit like trying to tell someone how to put up a deck chair. We are showing a sequence (which you might not want, or be able, to do all together) with some notes on each.

Rear entry is a whole scene. The
kneeling–lying positions with the
woman's hips raised give very deep
penetration and contact with her
whole perineum and buttocks. They
are also fine for adapting different-
sized partners. If he fails to get
enough friction he should hold his
penile skin back with one hand.
Enough symbolisms to fill a book, but
they are meant to be enjoyed. Rear
entry also works well flat or near-flat,
or you can fool around and make it
acrobatic

Close astride position. He is at her breasts baby-style, and holds back his foreskin to get more friction and shallower penetration

Woman astride. She has total body and breast contact and he can caress her buttocks

Sociable, but only a good orgasm
position if she has pelvic muscle
control. Immensely popular in
cultures which cultivate the latter –
Arab and Indian in particular

When she leans back (usually as she
gets toward orgasm) they get maximum
visibility and muscle tension

This Indian-Tantrik position is arduous, but try it if you're the right heights. Fun to do, though perhaps more for meditation than orgasm

Wide open with full genital contact but shallow penetration. Tiring and not good for someone with a weak back unless he gives her full support

A rest position, reached from any
ordinary rear entry simply by lying
down. Her buttocks come to hand
and both can make enough
movement to keep erection

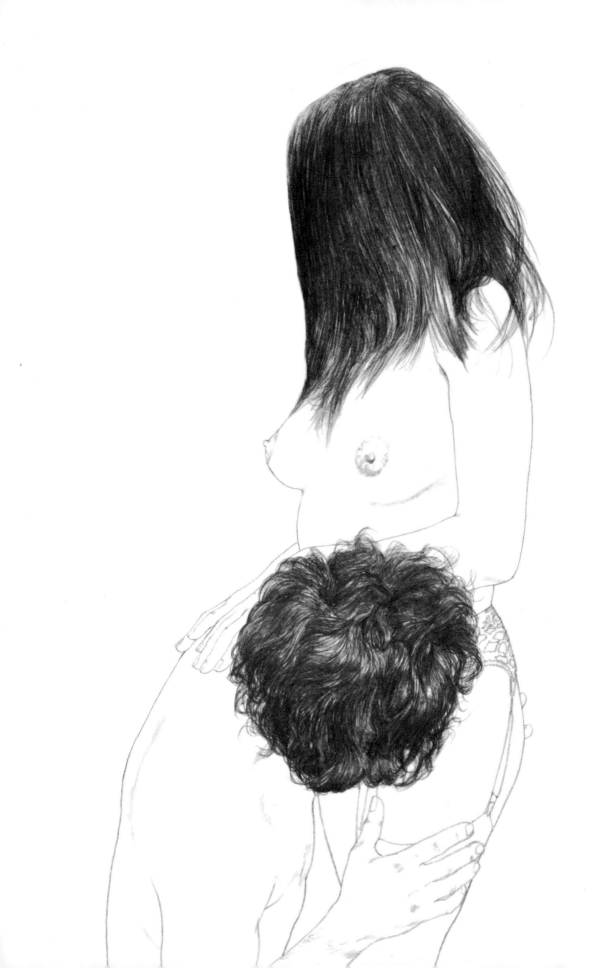

skin

The skin is our largest sexual organ, and the one through which we make close-range contact with any love object, as we did with our mothers in babyhood. If it has a language it's one of tender sensuality. For this reason generations of "gray" culture have tabooed it. They couldn't wholly taboo genital sex, but at least we needn't admit the rest of our bodies to the operation, or we might become genuinely sensual and value trust, pleasure and touch instead of fearing them and being guilty about them. There are still people around who've had fertile sex but never touched another person's skin, or let their own be touched.

Quite apart then from lovers learning to touch one another, to enjoy skin sensation, and to turn each other on through it, there's good sense in the nude encounter setup in which you touch the skin of both sexes, to see how it feels, and let them touch yours, to see how that feels. Most cultures and all animals stylize their touching of other individuals, use it as a language, and confine it to meaningful contexts – but we've got a lot of leeway to make up. We are contact animals (which naturally touch each other rather than spacing out like many birds), and skin satisfaction is probably one of our most important infant experiences, though one on which, because of clothing, some generations have gone short.

Lovers touch each other anywhere, with fingers, skin, lips and tongue (and should devote some quiet sessions simply to this kind of exploration, enjoying the sight, feel, taste and smell of each other). Who touches whom socially is a matter of regional variation, like who kisses whom and where – cheek, forehead, hand, lips, all with different meanings. One nice thing about American women is that they aren't afraid to touch men socially; this has shifted from skin to clothing (tie straightening, for example), but is a step in the right direction and communicative not seductive. Men are intensely afraid of touching each other except in certain set situations, and most sensuality training provides the educative experience of two males feeling each other's naked skin.

It's probably best, as a turnon and for social use, to combine skin touching with some muscular stimuli such as massage (q.v.), for skin and muscle weren't programed to function separately. Don't forget that all human skin is visibly or invisibly hairy, and that the hairs can be stimulated. Touching in our culture gets sexual when the lips and tongue become involved: a passing touch on the genitals doesn't say the same thing. Try being touched blindfold or eyes closed by one or several people and with different textures – feathers, cloth and so on (one group we heard of specializes in cracking an egg and pouring it on you, but this sounds like an optional extra).

The point, however, is to boost your own skin awareness, and that is sensible enough. The best domestic measure is simply total nakedness in bed, though that is only a start, and not all people who sleep together naked have really developed the awareness of each other's skins. It's odd but true that you can tell from skin feel if a person's turned on, turned off, hostile, or whatever – probably from the tone of the small underlying muscles – but don't mistake being cold literally for being cold sexually, though they feel similar. You need to be warm to start this – climate and past Ice Ages may account for some human and northern hangups.

soul power It must be the oldest human conviction and anxiety that Others (black if you're white, white if you're black) are larger, more potent and generally better at sex than you are. It would in fact be pretty odd, given the diversity of people, if all black men were better or worse at anything than all white men, except perhaps hiding on a dark night; but humans are given to idiotic racial generalizations. The old chestnut about genital size is also bunk. It probably originated from white encounters with Africans in a hot, humid climate where the resting penis isn't shrunk by cold and the intrepid explorers were clothed and couldn't see their own equipment. This sort of nonsense is insulting to both black and white.

Where black people of both sexes undoubtedly do score sexually is that Black culture has never lost its body sense as White has and isn't physically uptight. Its body language is much freer and accordingly many black people are better at sex than anxious Wasps for the same reason that they dance much better. Some degree of soul, rhythm and body sense is something we others badly need to relearn.

technique Don't be scared of technique – "reducing sex to a matter of technique" and so forth and so on. Sex is about total body communication between affectionate people. If you concentrate wholly on technique, try to show off, or think that because your line in tongue or finger work freaked out one person it will freak out another, you're missing this: *part* of the knowhow (the most important for tenderness) is reading the other person's responses and knowing what to do and what not to do, as well as signaling your needs to them. But if you don't know the ways in which the body can be explored – not just in theory, but how exactly – you haven't the equipment to be adaptable with.

This adaptability is one use of techniques. Most books are written as if people were morally and physically like an endless series of identical twins. In fact no two are alike. With a new partner the exploration is total, and you may be reading and meeting for the first time needs he or she didn't ever know about before. With a steady partner, technique comes into its own, because with easier and constant communication you can devote part of your lovemaking to perfecting everything which you both enjoy – getting your manual and oral techniques absolutely right for one another, working through postures and so on.

It's not cold-blooded to do this systematically, using about half your lovemaking, and let the rest run free, declaring, say, National Rear Entry Week or National Woman on Top Week every so often, looking for sensations you've missed. Some of these won't work for you, but don't write them off until you're sure it's preference and not inexperience which makes them fail. Both of you look out intelligently for love-gifts for the other – this can include things you learn from other people, from books, or from an active erotic imagination. Don't keep switching around for its own sake, but don't let sex get routine or it can stop being exploration of each other's bodies as well as communication between them. The range of skin, muscle, genital and oral sensations appropriate to all moods and needs within a good couple is near-inexhaustible: if you did exhaust it you'd need to start over, like painting the Bay Bridge.

One justification for having a threesome or an exchange sometimes is that it freshens this sense of continuing exploration. Practice so you can do everything quickly, expertly, unclumsily and without holdups and letdowns, but (especially if you're a man) not with a touch which communicates slick routine. Given this sensitivity, only in-out sentimentalists knock technique. Mostly they are folk who have none, with disappointed partners who've given up hoping for any.

The start of good sex is knowing what resources turn some people on and roughly why. If you have a lot of partners you need to start with this knowledge and can check it in practice. If you have one partner you can check parts of it – high skin response, high muscle erotism, whether or not they respond to oral work and so on – and concentrate accordingly. But store the other

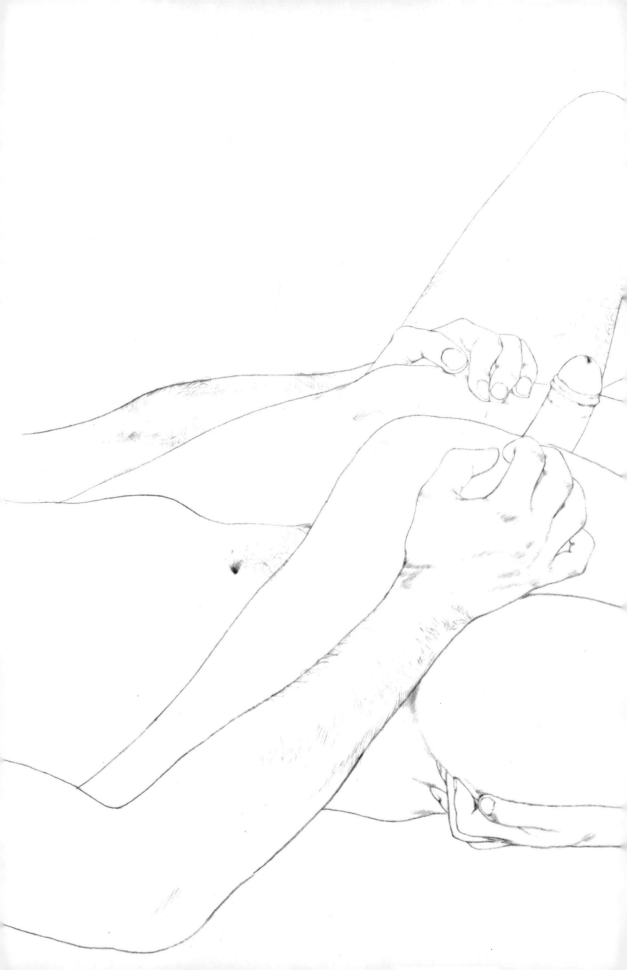

approaches. Someone who has become aware of his muscles may need to become aware of his skin for balance, and vice versa. The sex fantasies we have and volunteer represent known parts of ourselves, and a great deal of creative sex lies in exposing and developing others. So neither of you stick to known preferences except in let-go situations. Have these often, but intersperse them with deliberate experiment.

watching

Watching other people having sex is, for many couples, not only exciting but immensely instructive. (See *Sharing*.) Sex is about the only social skill we don't learn by watching: instead "gray" society has imposed ideas of modesty and privacy which imply that sex itself ought to be hidden and that other people are hostile. The result is individuals who worry if their performance, methods and tastes are normal and have had no way of checking this and no way of bettering their play by observation. You can learn more in one session by watching a few other couples than out of this whole book. If they know no more than you, you'll at least be turned on and reinforced about your abilities; if they are better at things like skin stimulation, or more creative over play, go and do likewise. Films are occasionally worth seeing, though a lot of porno directors and actors aren't enjoying themselves too much (see if the men get solid erections and the women a chest flush at orgasm – they can't fake that). But the shared scene with real people is naturally better, and you can talk as well. Some couples encourage friends to make love with them, even if they don't want to swing, simply so that they can all watch and compare styles – it's a good way to learn about sexual behavior. Most of the people who have written about sexuality never saw a couple making love – probably not even Sigmund Freud; it wasn't his scene. It's a heavy thought. How many books about football, telling you exactly how you should play it, have been written by people who never actually saw a game? It's a good question to ask any medical authority who pontificates about sex. We'd get less hogwash written.

Yes, we've watched dozens of couples, and a lot of the comment in this book is from direct observation. But don't take our word for it, try it and form your own conclusions. Watching yourself in a mirror is good but isn't the same exercise – you get no new information and no standard of comparison. Sex techniques are as varied as people – most of the nonsense in past books simply couldn't have survived even minimal direct observation. Watching and being watched is exciting, friendly and encouraging – not intrusive or embarrassing.

wrestling

Wrestling is sexually exciting. Quite a few people of both sexes are turned on by watching professionals – or the anthropoids who appear on television in Britain on Saturdays – chucking each other about. Most of us tried wrestling the other sex when we were kids: a lot of lovers enjoy wrestling. The trouble here is that in most couples it's not an equal match – in childhood one could get over this through age-difference, but the numerous males who are turned on by struggling with a woman as strong or stronger than they are may have mate-selection problems, because desirable wrestling partners don't necessarily make the best social or sexual choices on other counts. Even non-sexual struggling produces penis and nipple erection at least to half-staff in most young adults, as Classical artists knew.

If you don't mind the man winning most times, fine.

No biting, scratching or kicking is a wise rule if you want to stay sexually excited and not get hurt, but this does handicap the woman. If she needs to win or he to lose sometimes, handicap him – the wrestling princess in the Arabian Nights could beat men by magic, so you agree your own magic. Or make it a numbers game – after three defeats she has the right to take him prisoner and set up her own bondage scene. (See *Muscles*.) Silly? No more so than other kids' games: some couples simply don't relate by struggling, often because they haven't tried it. Others find loving struggle a turnon and – oddly, if you take "struggle" at its usual social value – wholly tender, a dramatization of trust as well as of complicated but quite normal needs to overpower, be overpowered, be or play at being the stronger or weaker. Kids use struggle to test their actual strength, lovers to experience feelings about strength in the relations of the sexes which they can't verbalize but which deepen their sense of identity and sharing. Being less strong than a woman is sometimes important to very strong males, and being stronger than a man on occasion lets girls try a part of the male role for size.

Never let struggling get spiteful, stop if it becomes rougher than either wants, don't do it if it seems pointless or turns you off, but try it – sensibly – if the idea excites you. If it's working, the tender element will be enough to prevent accidents. Even real fights can end this way – see the marvelous set-to in the movie *A Touch of Class* for a very well-observed scene of this sort.

His &
Hers

aggression

Most people in our culture are scared of aggression. It sounds like something which will set the United Nations dropping napalm on us, and we're indoctrinated against it, women especially. Symposia are held by medicos and welfare people on how to deal with it. In fact it's the most sloppily used word in social science, which is saying a great deal. At different times and in different mouths it means at least three things.

The first of these is hostility, the wish to clobber somebody. Clobbering people indiscriminately, either by hand or with bombs, is obviously a bad thing, but we needn't be ashamed of the purely domestic wish if it's reasonable. All lovers want to hit each other sometimes. One long-

term couple, asked if they'd ever considered divorce, replied: "Divorce never – murder frequently." This is absolutely normal.

The second meaning is assertion, wanting to make an impact on the environment – like an "aggressive" salesman or "attack" in music. One and two get mixed up not only verbally but attitudinally. Kids who feel that they are nonentities entirely surrounded by solid granite corporation offices attack people or break up property by way of making an impact quite as much as out of hostility. Pre-lib women had the problem that while men were expected, as a male performance, to be aggressive in the second sense, and often aggressive in the first sense to back it up, any attempts by women to be aggressive in the second sense were taken as aggressive in the first and put down. There is a biological relationship, of course, in that the first is often the backup when the second, which all but the most timid humans need, is frustrated.

There's also a third component related to both these – dominance. This is a zoology term for a behavior by which animal societies are quite often ordered, where some individuals defer to others more dominant, so forming a "peck order," and it generates still more verbal confusion. Basically dominance in Man means the ability to relate confidently and unanxiously to other individuals and know, intuitively and by reading nonverbal sjgnals, what role to adopt towards them. It has absolutely nothing to do with "domination," either socially or as a sexual charade. People who have to wear jackboots and crack whips aren't relating confidently to others: they need a whole range of props in order to relate at all. The same goes when the domination is real, by way of social or domestic bluster.

One prevailing theory about aggression-hostility is that you can store it up, like garbage on a camper, and dump it at intervals. It's by no means certain that this is the case, but a lot of therapy has been based on having people take out accumulated hostility on cheap crockery, rubber dummies, or by bashing one another with pillows or batacas. Clearly a low-dominance subject (or a person in a dicey situation) who daren't show anger to a spouse or a boss may go and kick the cat, but this is less a process of storage than one of passing on one's resentment down the dominance line. Jumping up and down or smashing things are classical chimp demonstrative behaviors, and represent nonverbal expression of what we can't trust ourselves to say (for a direct view of chimp behavior, watch a footballer who just dropped a pass, and compare the expressive phrase "hopping mad"). Where dummy-bashing and bataca-fighting help is probably in teaching us not to be afraid of our own emotions.

Maslow, who studied dominance and sexuality in women, divided dominance into feeling (self-esteem) and status (being more or less strong or adequate than some other person). The only relationship between high domi-nance and aggression is that people with a high level of self-esteem are less blocked about expressing anger when they feel it – others keep quiet for fear of the con-sequences. High self-esteem in Maslow's women went with a rejection of many male-prescribed feminine per-formances like timidity, submissiveness, religiosity and conservatism, and with high enjoyment of genuinely feminine sex – orgasm, equal relations, experimentation. High-dominance women also had a positive attitude to sex generally, not being scared to come on top, not because they wanted the man to be underneath but because they enjoyed it that way. Where both parties had this high self-esteem, Maslow wrote, "every aspect of sex and sensuality is eagerly, enthusiastically accepted and warmly thought of . . . experiments of all kinds are made, all sexual acts are thought of as 'fun,' rather than as a serious business. Very frequently in a marriage between high-dominance people there has been experience of every form of sexual behavior known to the psycho-pathologist as well as the sexologist. . . . These acts [anal intercourse, homosexual contacts, oral sex, exhibitionism, group sex, etc.] have no pathological tinge nor are they pathogenic in any way. . . ." In other words, a high-dominance couple tries everything once and enjoys the lot, as fun and without fear.

Great, if you can do it, but we aren't all, and don't have to be, high-dominance people, and both halves of a couple are seldom equally self-confident, sexually or otherwise. It doesn't matter if there is a stronger party, and which is stronger in a particular situation is apt to vary. The point is that while the high-dominance person can learn to turn it down and play it tender on occasions (and would miss a whole section of sexual fulfillment if they didn't), they are the only people to get the best out of playful sex. Since a high proportion of folk are blocked in their capacity for sensuality by fears, better-not feelings, and the attempt to use love as an adhesive rather than an experience, training in reasonable assertion (aggression two) can help their sex lives, and the kind of gourmet attitude to sex which we've described can help their capacity for assertion. Very low-dominance and put-down people can react by overasserting and becoming Napoleonic bullies. Usually this shows because it also involves a lot of hostility (aggression one).

Types of sexual play are important as well. Low-dominance women regard coming out on top and other things such as digital-clitoral orgasm as "untender": they might be advised to try these things more often. Some people enjoy aggressive-looking games, either because they enjoy the try-everything self-confidence they know they have, or because it helps them to dramatize a self-confidence they haven't. A few are quite disablingly stuck with them. On the other hand, don't overdo the symbolic interpretation of turnons. For most people who enjoy struggling, bondage, simulated rape, and other non-cruel and non-dangerous "aggressions," they aren't aggressive at all, or even very symbolic, but depend quite simply on the physical kicks involved, with some references to childhood ideas of sex roles thrown in. Quite often, if they dramatize anything, it isn't aggression but trust, and overcoming the idea that the other sex is a bit dangerous.

It has been found too that women who like sadistic-looking games in which they play at dominating the male often aren't sadistic, in the correct sense of getting pleasure from hurting or humiliating someone. They are simply trying the conventional, phoney, overaggressive male role for size to see what it feels like, and to experiment at the same time with the sensation of being the stronger partner. The idea of masculinity in which he "dominates" her, by force and socially, is long out of date, but there's no harm in seeing what it would have felt like, in a secure pattern. Men who dramatize dominating women are more often trying to get over the idea that females are basically dangerous. If you have these needs, incorporate them into play and take turns – they have nothing to do with cruelty or hostility.

In any case, "being overpowered" and "being penetrated" do have a biology for women, but high-dominance women treat them as kicks and aren't frightened or devalued by them. Between self-confident people if either does any physical submitting on a given occasion it's in the interest of mutual orgasm and treated as fun, not violation, and part of a wholly equal and tender rough-and-tumble, interspersed with many much more gentle and relational passages. For them a totally unaggressive, tenderness-obsessed male who takes no initiatives without asking is a dead turnoff, as is a totally non-initiative-taking, non-penis-seizing woman. The temptation is to try to excite hostility in such a partner if you can't get any other sort of response, and needle them until they do something, even if it's only to shout.

Accordingly, "aggression" in loveplay is a good part of the human sex repertoire and only a danger-signal if it gets out of hand. As to real hostility, it's best dealt with by expressing frank anger at the time, and discussion (not nagging, sulking, no-saying or finding ways of getting even) afterward – that is, if you are adult adults.

The final attribute of low-dominance people, and perhaps, as Maslow came to think, the most important one, is insecurity. They don't express hostility or anger because they are afraid of being rejected, or that the partner will go away. Because they are using him or her as a stick to climb up, even the possibility that they might have to start on their own, that a relationship might not live happily ever after, and that they might have to be individuals is too frightening to contemplate. For these people permanence is a fetish, other people are sources of essential vitamins, and love involves possession or annexation.

This, as you will see from what we've said, makes a whole circle, because it turns relationship into a form of aggression: it is aggressive (and devaluing) to own someone, to impose rules on them, and so on. All people need other people. For high-dominance folk, love is an experience between people. If it is good they hope it will last. If it ends they will experience mourning, but not lose their self-esteem. They also tend to value experiences as they happen and not as guarantees that they will last forever: none do, if only because people are mortal. For low-dominance people love is often semiparasitic possession. Immediate joy is lost in worrying or planning ways to make sure it lasts and putting out more tentacles.

These are Maslow's "being-love" and "deficiency-love." Blake expressed it better:

> He who bends to himself a joy
> Doth the wingéd life destroy:
> He who catches joy as it flies
> Lives in eternity's sunrise.

Most of us share both the need for joy and the need for some kind of security – this is only reasonable. But it's worth pondering how love gets turned into aggression by low self-esteem people, and how high self-esteem people turn hostility into love through play. Frederick Perls put it best: "I am I and you are you, and neither of us is here to live up to the other one's expectations. But if we meet it's beautiful." Tigger was a high-dominance person, Eeyore a low-dominance person. Pooh comes between the two, on the low side.

boys

The two chief attributes of boys in our culture are that they carry a colossal load of male-expectation ideas, and that they are physically more easily excited to the point of no return than are girls. The first of these makes them extra-vulnerable to the restarting, by any kind of put-down, of childhood anxieties about being competitive and virile (girls are vulnerable to different things – though both are vulnerable to the idea of being rejected). Consequently they tend to be muscle-and-penis centered, or to make up in other ways for not being so. The knowledge that he has made it with a girl "feels different" from the girl's sensations on having made it with a boy – he has done the penetrating, she has let him in. Women's Lib may be changing this, but it's pretty basic.

The main thing about boys' responses is that girls are often unaware just how fast a really horny boy can be turned on; inconveniently fast, sometimes, if they don't know their own minds. Others end in bed because they can't believe that they are so desirable as to produce such an uncontrollable response. Quite a few cock-teasers don't intend to be so, they just don't know enough boy physiology: the sight of nice breasts and a few kisses will produce an erection in most males. If this happens and she doesn't want intercourse, she should tell him she has her period and offer an alternative. A boy can be given an orgasm by hand and if she doesn't know how, she should let him show her.

erection

Male erection can, of course, happen spontaneously, from being randy, seeing a sexy woman, a picture, etc., but it doesn't have to. Quite a lot of males at any time, most males at some times, and all males as they get older, do need direct physical stimulation of the penis to get fully hard, and will either stimulate it themselves or want their partner to do so. Worth saying because there are women who feel devalued if their man doesn't instantly erect "no hands" (and will make him flaccid for the whole session by saying so), and men who think it is somehow unmanly to ask for a rub when they need one. Both these attitudes arise from ignorance of human natural history.

The spontaneous erections which males get on waking and during periods of what is called "rapid eye movement" sleep (r.e.m.) are physiologically interesting: what sets them off is not known. The best thing to do with the morning kind is to use it there and then.

exhaustion

Something it seems almost impossible to get over to males. They get tired, and may be turned off sex by being preoccupied or anxious to a not-tonight-Josephine level, but never seem to be totally exhausted. For a start they find furious sex invigorating; and when very tired, they expect the woman to take over and rub, ride, suck or otherwise nurture them along to orgasm. But women do get genuinely exhausted, not least if, as is happening a lot in our culture, they're either expected to do two jobs, one

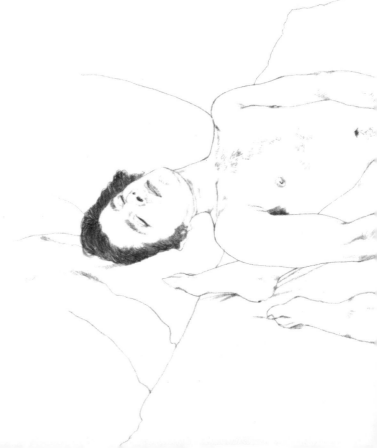

domestic and one other, or are subject to 24-hour child-demand.

Male folklore still seems to demand that the woman be at the bedroom door when he gets home, mouth open and contraceptive in place, horny as a bitch and loving with it, before leaving him to relax and getting the dinner. Afterward they make love at intervals all night and then she has to get up without waking him and fix coffee. This, it might as well be said bluntly, is not on. It may be a caricature but it's not far from the truth, and men who implicitly take the line that they do the work and all they're asking her to do is to keep the house clean and open her legs invite physical assault.

The facts are that women need sleep, and women with jobs and/or children need a lot of it. They don't respond well sexually when tired, and aren't easily able to get an orgasm then. If they do, it has a far more sedative effect than in men, and they usually need to rest and collect themselves – at which time they appreciate someone else dealing with children, getting coffee and so on, after a suitable period of togetherness. They can't convincingly deliver any of the wilder or more active sexual performances when tired.

All of this can be dealt with by a mixture of consideration and communication, unless adjustment is economically impossible and both must work flat out to stay afloat. Even then the situation can be improved, but not if men see fatigue (which they often use themselves to give them a letout for potency anxieties) as a covert sort of rejection, and exhaustion as sexual malingering. It's great on a vacation to wake her every time you have an erection, but if she works you have to be considerate. Even a token sharing of home jobs helps to take the pardonable resentment out of the situation: real consideration with frank discussion helps a lot more.

When she's exhausted and he isn't, lovemaking can be in order, but the main part of it will be holding her and not pushing the specifically sexual part unless she seems to need it. When he's exhausted and she isn't, it might be the time for this too, or for her to be very active: play it as it comes. Exhaustion is neither ignored nor denied between really loving people.

gay or straight

If a Martian was writing a history of human idiocy, he'd start with sexual behavior, and quite probably right here. All human beings are able in some circumstances to relate sexually to members of their own sex as well as to the other. This is probably true of most other mammals (though these use homosexual-looking behaviors for special purposes). It is only odd or anomalous biologically if, like some theologians, you think that reproduction is the only function of sex: in Man and many apes it isn't – bonding, or the expression of dominance, are equally important uses of what we regard as mating.

In all societies and at all times, a certain proportion of people have related more easily, or preferentially, to their own sex and not to the other. This behavior has been differently received. In some cultures it has been simply an accepted variation which anyone might move into and out of: Spartan or Japanese warriors balled their squires on campaigns, and thereby bonded them into the warrior group; classical Athenians reckoned that men should have one kind of sexual relation with boys and another kind with women. In others, the preference made one a wizard. Our own, influenced by Jewish fears of the "unnatural" and Christian hatred of sex generally, has hanged, burned, tortured and persecuted for centuries anyone who was rash enough to express this preference in action, or even in words. We have only just quit doing this. Homosexuals overlapped with witches and heretics, excited the same fears, and got similarly treated.

After hundreds of years of idiotic persecution, it's no wonder that people aware of similar preferences today have started Gay Liberation and demanded the right to do their own thing. Of course they have a right, but the campaign is unfortunate in that it reinforces the totally erroneous idea that there are two kinds of people, straight and gay (older apologists even insisted that gay people represented a third sex). The fact is that all people are both straight and gay if they'd let themselves be; the differences of emphasis have been stamped on by society's heaviest boots so that people are forced into an either/or choice instead of the subtler range of options which are really open to them. Society hasn't bothered too much about the same classification in women, nor persecuted them about it, and in consequence they show much more of the range of normal options and aren't nearly so bothered about relating to both sexes, affectionately and physically.

Some males would call themselves emphatically gay. They prefer relating to, and having sex with, men. This doesn't mean they have a response which others haven't. It means that they don't or can't relate to women. The why of this isn't known – learning, family experience and possibly genetics and prenatal hormone exposure may all play a part, and the convention that if you're one thing you can't be the other hasn't helped. A predominantly gay male who wanted to become heterosexual (some do, if it's a bad trip for them or they feel they are missing an important range of experiences) wouldn't need help to stop being attracted by men, for this is an unused potential present in all straight men which they've trodden on under orders from society. He would need help in overcoming his nonrelation with women.

The totally normal or zero-input state for unpropagandized, unintimidated males and females would probably be like that of the Classical Athenians – they'd be bi, able to relate sexually to men and women, but having individual preferences. It's not quite as simple as that, because man-man relations don't have the same biological functions as man-woman relations. People who insisted on treating contented homosexuals instead of torturing them to make their "abnormal" behavior "normal" were actually trying to make their behavior fashionable. But the repertoire of man-man responses, which obviously aren't connected with reproduction, are connected with dominance and with bonding: situations like the bonding between David and Jonathan can get sexual play added on because humans sexualize nearly everything. This looks odd to us, because in our panic over the supposed unmanliness of being gay we've suppressed all tenderness between males. A David and Jonathan who were affec-

tionate in the way our culture outlaws, but some others don't, would naturally use some companionate sex play to express it. (If you bridle at males being allowed to be mutually affectionate, stop and ask yourself why.)

Society being what it is, and our upbringing being what it has been, it's probably not a good idea for straight males (or bisexually aware males who have a settled hetero-sexual pattern) to rush out and realize all their bisexual potentials, simply because they might, unless they're very hardy, find it disturbing themselves and they would excite the hostility of disturbed people. One can't change one's culture overnight. They could however look at those potentials and notice the taboos on male-male affection they've been living by. People of either sex who are aware of their gay side, especially if they're adolescent, should be careful not to be hocused by society and by gay solidarity into taking a position, closing all other options, and settling to be gay for life. Apart from anything else, young people of both sexes often go through a normal period of relating better sexually to their own than to the other sex. If you settle to be gay you're foreclosing on options like reproduction, marriage and straight sexual experience, which are rewarding unless you really don't or can't use them; you're also buying a continuing underhand hassle from "garbage" people generally. It's quite possible to have both kinds of experience, and a bad thing to be totally blocked for either, especially for the sake of a name. You don't have to line up with either battalion – the flags are phoney anyhow.

In ordinary sex relations the sanest rules seem to be: don't upset a good and stable pattern when you've got it simply to realize a potential that hasn't mattered to you before; and don't be scared or upset in group scenes if you find yourself responding sexually to someone of your own sex. The latter is wholly normal and won't alter your existing pattern, only discharge some needs you hadn't realized (but don't equally do anything which will upset you or your partners after the excitement subsides). If you've got real needs, face them.

We didn't include gay sex in *The Joy of Sex*. Males use mutual hand and oral work and sometimes (not always, in spite of Sodom and Gomorrah) anal intercourse. Women use manual, oral and breast work, embracing, and sometimes mutual genital friction. The techniques are the same as in man-woman relations and so are the extras, but a same-sex partner often has a better idea of his or her partner's physiology and uses it very effectively, a thing people with gay experience sometimes miss in straight relationships. If you want your other-sex responses boosted for any reason, behavior therapy can help – but that is learning a new skill, not treating a disease. The whole range of human sex responses is normal and healthy: a less hungup generation will probably use more of it without being anxious.

giving head

Genital kisses are only a problem because they have become a male expectation and some otherwise sexy women are genuinely put off, not by doing it, but by the idea. One gets "he expects it, I find it really difficult – do women really enjoy it or is that male propaganda?" They do indeed enjoy it, not only for their partner's response, but for the sensual part of the experience – the texture of the penis, the sensuality of their own mouths, and often the ejaculation – which mixes up babyhood with a particular adult intimacy and a feeling of receiving. All of which is hardly surprising, in that it's a universal mammalian caress (so much for it being unnatural) and the male probably has an odor pheromone to turn on the female.

On the other hand, all heavy expectation is a bad thing and leads to rejection feelings if what turns one partner on turns the other partner off. Often the distaste hangup is boosted by lack of reciprocity: he wants her to give head, but won't do it himself, and is basically as distaste-concerned as she is, though he often won't admit this and gives some other reason. Really there shouldn't be pressure on anyone to adopt any form of sex behavior – only encouragement not to miss good ones.

Oral sex has come from bad magic to an obligatory sign of sexual turned-on-ness in ten years flat. All the same there are still some clown-made state laws which constitute it a felony. (It's hard to imagine sane legislators sitting down and seriously prescribing which part of your man or woman you may kiss.) The genitals have only just stopped being "dirty" on the sayso of generations of parents, nursemaids and schoolteachers, so it isn't surprising if some people still have problems. In people who don't wash, including some of both sexes, they are dirty, and are distasteful to kiss, like the mouths of folk who don't attend to their teeth.

Good oral sex isn't only a supreme love-gift to a partner but a potential turnon to the giver, and it is one of the sex experiences which it would be a pity to miss unless it really turns you off. Getting rid of any needless hangup isn't helped if you read hung-up psychiatrists who suggest that it's humiliating and really appeals to maso-chists (they say the same about women who like inter-course from behind). It's worth overcoming that prejudice. Make him wash if he doesn't. There really isn't much dif-ference, except in the mind, between operating on a clean penis and on a thumb, so practice on a thumb. It helps to get it mutual – say "my turn now" and push his head in the right direction. But don't run any part of your sex on a basis of "if you won't, I won't." If it's the ejaculation part which you dislike, skip that. And remember, if you have been turned off this and you suddenly do it unasked, the response is likely to be well worth the effort. It might never be your favorite sex play, but a penis is one of the world's two best playthings. Most women who give good head do it because they find it intensely enjoyable themselves, not because a demanding or insensitive man lays it on them. It's also a situation in which they have total control, not a kind of household chore.

Another consequence of male expectation is that some males expect oral sex to be the ultimate. If they don't reach orgasm with it they may say you don't know how to do it. In fact, over a quarter of males can't regularly be brought to orgasm in this way without added hand work, however skilled the operator: this includes many who have frequent sex of other kinds and simply need more friction than the tongue and lips can provide. It's worth knowing this.

As to the male side, the only reason good muff-diving hasn't become an overt female expectation leading to identical male hangups is that women have kept unreasonably quiet about their needs for fear of a bad reception. All women who have ever experienced good genital kisses will come to expect them, many who haven't would like them, and reading and franker discussion about sex will equalize the situation in which males have done the demanding until recently. There's been even more ignorant support from psychological literature here for the idea that kissing a woman's vulva is an act of submission and so on. In a good scene all genital kisses are totally mutual. She should wash (fruit essence and other muck isn't a help), but beyond that any distaste problems are in the mind and shouldn't outlive a single trial.

The clean genital odor of both sexes is a built-in stimulus. If it is distasteful, something is wrong. She should ask when she wants it – with some males it's no good waiting for initiatives. He should be prepared, moreover, to develop a lot of technique. It's no good working for five minutes and then saying "It's my turn now." Unlike men, some women can take a full half-hour, with intercourse afterward. As these are some of the most rewarding things in sex, for both sexes, it's well worth both of you making yourselves virtuoso performers.

his and hers

There are plainly biological differences between men and women – if there weren't there wouldn't be this book – but beyond the really obvious ones, the most striking thing is that among the real and the supposed behaviors and aptitudes which our culture rates as male or female, it's virtually impossible to tell which are built in and which aren't. Women might really be biologically better at intuition (meaning the ability to read nonverbal signs) or they might just have been expected to be so socially and acquired the skill. There might be a built-in reason for the predominance of male composers and painters, or it might be similar to the predominance of non-Eskimos in Congress. Even if you start arguing that men have masterpieces because women have babies, and prefer having them, you also start with a set of assumptions laid on women by a society which told them to prefer babies. Now babies aren't compulsory, more women will get time and opportunity to compete – Bach didn't have to blow the noses of his tribe of children, and the only organ Mrs Bach can have had time for was her husband's.

Almost all the subtler differences in actual response between men and women in our society are of this "probably learned" kind. In fact, we know from children brought up in the wrong sex that sex roles, and even biological-looking things like activity and choice of aggressive or non-aggressive play, are about 80 per cent learned, though hormone levels can and do affect behaviors in male and female directions. The social override in man is absolutely enormous.

We learn, therefore, to be masculine or feminine according to the rules laid down by society. As those rules change, so will the expectation that is imposed on a child as it learns its sex role. Our kids may be learning that the roles of the sexes in society are similar, and so grow up like racehorses – where the sexes look much alike and the odds on a horse and a mare are about equal. It ought to be obvious from this that there are no set human sex roles – each period forms and transmits its own. Women may be expected to scream and faint or to land with airborne troops, men to dominate women and treat them as slaves or to defer to them totally. It depends when you lived and where (though at any time there would have been people of either sex who welcomed their role or detested it). On the whole the gentle and sexuality-centered societies have struck a more reasonable balance based on affectionate equality with some variety.

We don't want here to go much into the social aspects of male and female equality because it's been widely discussed. The biological differences do remain, and are interesting. The first and most obvious is that the male gets an erection, whereas the woman lets him in. This can affect, and has affected, the attitudes of both (see *Penetration*, *Performance*), but it does so a great deal more in the traditional male-chauvinist setup than between people who have a different, less polarized attitude, and have learned to make love with their whole bodies. How much we build on top of a biological fact depends on how strongly we feel – and are hung up – about it.

Second, women can bear and suckle children and men can't. Moreover men aren't programed to nurture very young babies, because they lack the subcutaneous fat which provides the appropriate body texture, and this probably matters more than having or not having milk. It's also possible that they don't smell right. Our culture has bypassed some of this in that neither sex nurtures babies much when naked, though, from what we know of ape biology, it might be better if they did. It may also once have been important that a woman didn't have a beard which would conceal her facial expression.

A much more important fact is that today women "can" have babies: not so long ago it was a "must." Now that motherhood is a matter of total choice, sex can be recreational, not reproductive, at will. This is the greatest single factor in making the needs and experience of men and women more alike and more equal. Compulsory pregnancy – the sanction behind most of the other putdowns – is the main thing women have been liberated from. "Unfulfilled biological drives toward motherhood" which go beyond liking children and wanting to have one usually represent, like Kant's categorical imperatives, something the person learned before they were five, and are due to what mother said or did, not to hormones or Jungian fairies.

Thirdly, women's hormonal patterns are cyclical and men's aren't. Apart from the fact that magic about menstruation has been a prime source of female putdowns since the Stone Age, this is important, because the hormone cycle measurably affects intellectual and physical performance and mood, as athletes and examination candidates know to their cost. Most suicides and impulsive crimes among women occur in the few days preceding a period – in men, they're spread regardless of time – but though cyclical things like epilepsy, migraine and depression often synchronize with the cycle, they aren't necessarily commoner than in males. At the same time we're going, if it becomes safely feasible, to see calls for menstrual suppression. This is sometimes done now even though it still looks a little risky.

Whether there are attitudinal differences, apart from those arising from having or not having these experiences, or aptitude differences apart from the roles men and women have learned to expect, we simply can't know

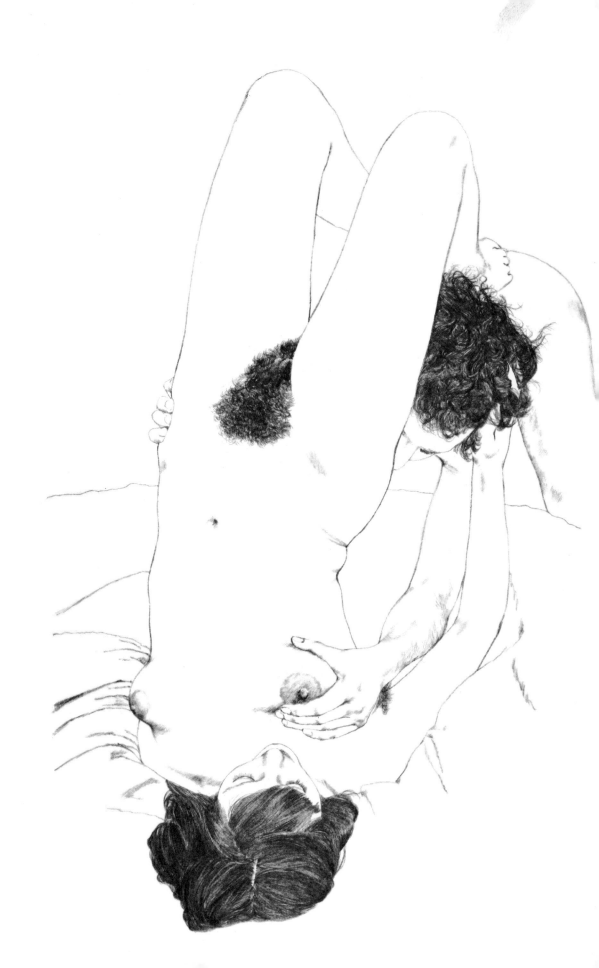

until both sexes start with more similar social roles, if then. If there are, they're probably complementary.

Between lovers, the differences which matter are the muscle difference and the texture difference – the texture of each sex delights the other, and here the reproductive-maternal echo is real and valuable. She has a nurturing surface and breasts, and she smells feminine – all men had mothers, and this is a delight. He has a texture different from her own, he is often strong enough to pick her up, and all women had fathers. Harmless, semi-seductive play with a father in infancy is known to be about the best guarantee that a woman will respond fully to men when adult, and a lot of that is in the prefiguring of male contact. It can also generate turnoffs if the reminiscence is wrong. Exploring these reactions before going on to the equally fascinating visual and tactile exploration of each other's genitals is one of the best parts of the interaction of man and woman.

mess

Two competing truths here: proper enjoyment of sex involves getting over the idea that the genitals, the secretions involved and the entire business – including the human body as a whole – are messy, dirty, unworthy or repugnant in any way. At the same time, sex is messy at a practical level and in our culture women, however liberated, have often in the past had to clean up, and frequently still do. Semen isn't filthy, but it's hard to get out of furnishings, or out of one's hair, and however good sex may be it's a comedown to wake up lying in a pool or to catch your man wiping his hands or his penis on your clean covers when you have put out a towel. Some feminine fastidiousness is pretty practical.

Split the problem, and make sensuality exercises practical too. Menstrual intercourse is fine, but have it somewhere that doesn't stain, like the shower. For other purposes make a sensible use of towels, but don't thrust one into the hands of a partner who has just had an orgasm, or wipe off semen so precipitately that it looks like rejection – strike a balance. In some situations, such as slow masturbation of the male, semen is bound to go all over the place (he may look as if he'll never stop ejaculating) and the waterworks are part of the woman's turnon. Here it's better to clean up afterward than try to slam a cloth over him and lose the last spurt. You could put a condom on him if it's essential to leave no traces, but you'll miss a part of the fun.

If you have to choose, it's more important not to entertain ideas that sex and any attendant stains are "dirty." But if the practical aspects become a putdown, use the same ingenuity you'd use in a motel where you don't want to be surcharged or embarrassed. Have drip-dry sheets on the sexual bed, and put a non-crackling plastic layer over the mattress (motels do this, and not for fear of enuretics). Pick semen-proof sexual furniture (so you don't have to break off and find something to put over a chair). How far you furnish your house, or a part of it, around sexual realities is a measure of how far you've come – and how often.

penetration

There is something basic in the fact that she has to let him in – not only on to her territory or into proximity, but actually into her body. There aren't many identifiable, built-in male-female differences, but this is one of them and it does affect feminine thinking. Sex is external to a man, located in an offshore peninsula like the State of Florida, and he puts forth; it's internal to a woman – a visit or an invasion – and she has something external left with her. This doesn't mean that women unconsciously see all intercourse as a violation; the fact of having the man inside can be warm, good and reinforcing as nothing else, but he's still what the lawyers call an invitee.

These emotions are complicated, and men wouldn't easily intuit them. Positive and negative feelings about being penetrated play quite a part in patterning women's actual response, and some rather enragé Women's Libbers have suggested that every man should himself be penetrated at least once to see what it feels like. We doubt that this would work fully – anal penetration isn't really programed and doesn't feel the same.

One spinoff is that women tend far more than men to regard the place they live as a body surrogate while men regard theirs as a territory. A woman who hates letting people into her apartment is saying something – so is the woman who says, "He should be happy with me, Doctor – I've made him a lovely home with wall-to-wall carpeting." She's really talking about her body.

Being deeply penetrated by a man you love and trust, who treats you as an equal and loves you back, is about the best of all feminine experiences – it marks the end of any anxieties about who is entering whom. At that point the penis is joint property and a lot of infantile fears get resolved.

performance

Another man-woman basic is that while she, at worst, can lie back and let sex happen, he needs a positive physiological response – erection. Given all the other male feelings of anxiety, which arise from the fact that the penis isn't only for balling, but is also a dominance signal like antlers, it's almost impossible for the man not

to regard erection as a performance, achievement, and general badge of masculinity. For people with any erectile problems this type of overanxious striving has the same effect as loud noises or a cold bath and makes relaxed erection nearly impossible. It's as if the Evolutionary Demon has fixed it so males can only show their dominance-signal (and reproduce) if they're confidently relaxed rather than hopped-up to impress – not a bad arrangement, but it leads to a lot of problems for some.

There's no sure way of altogether stopping males from regarding sex as a performance test. Probably the best plan is to shift their interest to something which matters, namely a sensitive ability to turn on and satisfy a woman with or without an erection. This performance is well worthwhile, and by taking off the heat it usually improves erection anxieties.

plenty of time

The one thing nobody realizes when they are adolescents is that there *is* plenty of time, and adults should point this out if they can – not that adolescents should turn down sensible opportunities for sexual experience just to please adults or to conform to adult expectations. At the same time the boy of 16 who listens to boys of his own and higher ages bragging about the girls they've had, or the girl whose classmates boast about dates, isn't irretrievably on the shelf, though it certainly feels that way at the time. The best advice if others are really scoring more social successes is: "Notice how they do it and why you don't. It's often because they have more confidence, which comes with age, and maybe they took the trouble to acquire social skills, like dancing."

Some of the worst confidence binds are appearance-centered – spottiness or overweight – and these, too, often cure themselves between 16 and 17. If they don't, they can be tackled, sensibly, later: the main thing is to see they don't damage sexual and personal self-esteem during important years and make a youngster over-shy or wildly promiscuous in an attempt to catch up. Note that the spottiest, fattest or plainest adults of both sexes acquire mates (tell them to look around at your dinner guests – they didn't all get like that in middle age).

Body anxieties are quite the most crippling sexual disabilities – in fact there's no body configuration which can't be offset by social skills like vivacity, humor and considerateness. These, however, need learning. Everyone is gauche at 16 and if your child spends time worrying about being left out he/she won't acquire them. It's unfortunate that all but the lucky among us meet most putdowns from equally callow classmates when we're least equipped to laugh them off. Learning to address the other sex as people (without showing off or being in a cold sweat, and above all without hurrying for fear someone more confident gets there first) is the most important skill. Adolescents shouldn't copy he-man or sex-siren approaches from classmates, who are probably quite as uptight inside as they are. In fact, they should realize that everyone feels insecure however studlike or beautiful or popular they are. Nobody tries to learn to ski in three weeks flat and love is a more complicated skill than skiing.

saying no

It's a by-product of the work that educators have done in the last few years to kill off hogwash-based notions of the dangerousness, guiltiness and unworthiness of sex that some people go to the other extreme and reverse their former anxieties. They worry that they aren't getting satisfaction when often they are, and they get guilty about saying no.

Between a couple who have regular sex it's just about the best test of the spontaneity of their relationship that either can say no when for some reason they don't really feel like sex, without anyone feeling guilty, rejected or being ostentatiously resigned. Women who are tired (see *Exhaustion*) and men who are preoccupied often agree to try and then resent it, or say no and then feel guilty. If someone says no all the time, of course, there's something wrong and you should investigate. But in a good couple either can do so when they mean no, and should agree to play it this way.

For singles, often young girls, it's a question of not being blackmailed or overpersuaded. The letter-column answer "if he wants to lay you, dear, he doesn't really love and respect you" is bunk. On the other hand, all normal men tend to want sex, at least in fantasy, with any woman they get close to, and this is even truer of boys who urgently need to prove their manhood and desirability. Girls need to feel desirable too, and there are complex emotions about not being rejected, not being left out, and so on. Routine yes-saying, however, isn't more rational than compulsive no-saying; it can lead to still more rejection if you use your body as a love-gift to lay an obligation on someone, and it's idiocy if you aren't 100 per cent baby-proof. The time to say yes is when you are fond of each other and both will enjoy it without strings or ensuing obligations. It's also better not to say yes out of sympathy. Agreeing to say yes on other terms, and especially to avoid loneliness, only works if you are strong-minded enough not to be disappointed if sex doesn't prove to be a contact adhesive and sustain the relationship.

It isn't only teenagers who need to learn to say no. One of the most valuable lessons learned by the women who went to Sandstone (q.v.) was precisely this.

security

It's part of psychiatric folklore that security acts as a releaser in women. This is by no means always true: there are quite a few women for whom danger or excitement are releasers – like the wife in *Une Femme Mariée* hugging herself in the taxi on the way to her lover each time she passed a Dangerous Corner sign. At the same time it's part true. In a recent study by Dr. Fisher a sense of security had a higher correlation with orgasm than any other sexual circumstance. What is probably true is that while insecurity is a turnoff in both sexes, society has laid socially secure partnership extra heavily on women as a prerequisite for enjoying sex. The things which make men insecure, on the other hand, except sexual nonperformance, don't enter the bedroom. Very dominant and self-esteeming women don't feel this so much, but most of them need either the stability of the relationship or a stable setup as background. Loss of the fear of pregnancy, which would be a sound biological background for a security need, might alter this.

Finally, for some people security lies not at the social level but simply in being at ease with the partner they have on that occasion, and the rightness or wrongness of their communication. For Maslow's findings on this, see *Aggression*.

selfishness

Some people might think that this is a prosperous middle-class book, meant to help prosperous middle-class white people experiment with sensuality, purely personal experiences and kicks in a world that is rapidly going to hell on wheels.

Quite the reverse is the case. Of course good sexual experiences are easier to achieve for prosperous people who have privacy, contraception, leisure and control over their lives. So is good medical care. But at the same time, acquiring the awareness and the attitudes which can come from this experience doesn't make for selfish withdrawal: it's more inclined to radicalize people.

The antisexualism of authoritarian societies and the people who run them doesn't spring from conviction (they themselves have sex), but from the vague perception that freedom here might lead to a liking for freedom elsewhere. People who have erotized their experience of themselves and the world are, on the one hand, inconveniently unwarlike–they'd rather stay and make love than kill Vietnamese or Hungarians–and, on the other, violently combative in resisting goons, political salesmen, racists and "garbage" people generally who threaten the personal freedom they've attained and want to see others share.

The obsession with money-grubbing and power-hunting is quite largely fueled by early distortions of body image and of self-esteem – distortions that carry over into a whole range of political behaviors, from hating and bullying people to wrecking the countryside for a profit you don't need and can't use. In fact, most great powers are now run by a minority of sick people, suffering from their inability to erotize and hence humanize their experience, who use the rest of us for play therapy. Somebody once challenged Marcuse, when he was arguing on these lines, "Go erotize the State of Kansas." That could be happening. Marcuse is an old-style Marxist who still sees Marxism as radical and laments the fact that existing Marxist bureaucracies are violently antisexual as well as antilibertarian in tone.

A generation that has erotized its experience will be radical in quite a different vein – environmentalist, science-based (because you need to study human biology to know why you function) and hopefully as ungovernable by non-people as the American Colonies were by King George. If your widened self-experience and experience of others leave you an unreconstructed Middletown don't-carer, it wasn't widened enough or human enough.

simultaneous orgasm

Great when it happens, but it is a hangup from modern sexual folklore that it has to happen every time or even often, and that you've fallen short if it doesn't. This differs as much as every other sexual attribute. Some couples always get there together, others sometimes or rarely, a few never, but this matters not a whit. Worth mentioning because the contrary is one of many counseling fantasies, due to the writing of sex books by people who haven't had much sex, or much variety of experience, themselves.

If you specially want it and want to try for it, the idea would be to time both partners' responses during your most usual pattern of lovemaking, then use some other technique before starting the ignition sequence for about the time you estimate it needs for the slower to catch up. This doesn't always work, as full arousal may depend on the usual pattern you've learned, but it may do, with adjustment. If the woman is the slower, the best thing to try is breast play followed by a long period of tongue work on the vulva (better than using the finger – a long genital kiss leaves her wet, and will slow him down when he goes in). If he's the slower, she can start with oral or hand work (building her own arousal at the same time), put him in astride to complete this, then they turn over, timing this if possible so that both are just into their home stretch, and can go at it flat out. If she can get several climaxes, he should with luck synchronize with one of these (the folklore doesn't seem to recognize that most women are or can be multiorgasmic).

size

Sex counselors, who aren't, and don't wish to appear, unsympathetic, are just about fed up with answering anxious people's questions about penile size. We've spent years telling enquirers, correctly, that penile size is, functionally, wholly unimportant; that most people who worry that they are smaller than other males aren't (they simply haven't seen other males in erection, at least since boyhood); that the only difference between penises which are large and small when flaccid, a few rare conditions excepted, is that the large kind enlarge less on

erection; and that imagination matters far more in love-making than a donkey-size dong. Open sex and mutual observation would cure a lot of this nonsense – large size may be idealized in Texas, but they do fine in New Hampshire, too.

The trouble is, however, that the anxiety isn't personal but programed. The penis is not only for putting in the vagina, but is also apparently a dominance signal in other primates. We don't, like squirrel monkeys, get an erection to warn off another male (or rather, there isn't any printed observation that we do, though primitives who greet by patting each other's penises look a bit as if they were checking that the other male isn't threatening), but we seem to have kept the wiring so that it forms our attitudes. Saying you are small compared with other males is a statement about your self-estimate. In fact we've probably moved the dominance-signal behavior into infancy, where Father is bigger than I am. One thinks of Cassius's remark about Caesar:

Why man, he doth bestride the narrow world
Like a colossus; and we petty men
Walk under his huge legs, and peep about
To find ourselves dishonorable graves.

One practical importance of this, and of feeling small in our relations with more-dominant males, is that if you feel small your penis will, as a result, actually retract when you are naked together, as it does in cold water – hence the vicious circle. Assertion training and warm weather will do more to give you a normal-sized resting penis than devices that increase the size of the makers' bank accounts. One or two good sex experiences will do still more. Women who put down a partner, either over resting size or over erection capacity, can upset unconfident people and would make bitchy partners anyway. It pays to recall that dominance isn't everything, and some kingsize flaccid penises attached to muscle-men stay flaccid at the moment of need, while many smaller specimens move briskly into an operating position.

vaginal orgasm

Some women's orgasms always feel the same, and some have an habitual pattern – one big one, or many, or a plateau in which they all run together. But even with an habitual pattern most women surprise themselves sometimes with one massive all-out climax when they usually plateau, or some other variation. Orgasms also feel different in both sexes when given in different ways, by hand or by mouth for instance. In women the clitoris and the surrounding tissues are the most usual trigger, but some find a direct stimulation of these too intense and prefer the incidental approach to them through deep penetration. Once in the mood, quite a few women can get orgasms from almost any region of the body – earlobes, breasts, fingers, soles of the feet – and even from listening to music or watching football. We know one woman who had to give up going to the hairdresser because brushing out gave her an orgasm. Luckily nobody has tried to classify all these.

Orgasms as turned-on people experience them are a little like the varieties of wine, and as hard to classify. Unfortunately, as always, the nonplaying coaches (chiefly male) have moved in: "clitoral" orgasms are immature, "vaginal" orgasms are unliberated and don't exist, etc. Apart from the fact that most of these writers can't have had a female orgasm and sound as if they have never witnessed one, they have caused a lot of anxiety in people who haven't yet learned that most admonitory writing about sex is hogwash. The best thing, if one thinks about it, is to enjoy your own pattern to the full and explore other responses to see if you can vary it.

The origin of the clitoral-vaginal hassle was in Freud's obsession with intromission as the only mature sexual activity, and his idea that the clitoris is a little penis, so that to be maturely female one had to "transfer" sensitivity to the vagina (which doesn't happen to have any sensory nerve endings). This seems to leave aside the question of what, in this case, the clitoris is for – a front door bell is there to be rung. Of course a mature female enjoys deep intercourse, and there are biological reasons for this if she's to reproduce, but Freud never appreciated the play functions of sex, and his idea of maturity was as rigid as the Catholic idea of virtue. The clitoris was installed to be enjoyed, and if it's your mascot, don't let theory worry you.

What does appear to be true is that some women, either always or sometimes, get a different, and often an even more overwhelming, sensation from quick intercourse without preliminaries but with very deep penetration, and distinguish this from the orgasm they get by clitoral stimulation or even by regular but less vehement intercourse. What seems to be happening here is that the trigger area is the peritoneum, the sensitive membrane lining the abdomen, not the vagina. This sort of orgasm produces gasping, breath-holding, and a once-for-all climax sensation, and women who know they can get either kind are often aware which, on a particular occasion, they want. Too much preliminary clitoral contact or foreplay seems to block this special response which, when it does happen, is as rapid as a man's. Subjective accounts may just mean that everyone's pattern of preference differs, but they need to be considered, even if there isn't much difference in the physiological changes – after all, the importance of an orgasm is how it feels, not its physiology.

If the peritoneum is sexually sensitive it could explain why anal intercourse works, in some members of both sexes: the only specifically feminine thing about this experience is that most men don't get penetrated routinely. It probably also explains why pressure on the abdomen can boost response in some women. But since not everyone does respond like this, it's pointless to feel disappointed if you don't.

Some very insecure women turn off to clitoral response altogether and find it nasty, oversharp or untender. Often this is a carry-over from masturbation fears, or not being able to relax sensually unless they have deep penetration, which reinforces the sense of "possessing" the partner and has maternal overtones they find reassuring. This might happen less if women and girls were encouraged to masturbate. Good masturbation enhances response by teaching the acceptance of sensuality, and doesn't impair any deep responses they may develop later. It's a pity to miss out on either. See *Masturbation and learning*.

weaker sex

Sexually speaking, the male. In consequence, over the centuries, he has tended to talk women into restricting their potential sex performance, a process in which women themselves have co-operated. What has put paid to this has been the final separation of sex from reproduction: women now can realize their full sexual potential without anxiety, they can swing if they wish. Above all they can accept the fact that for both sexes sexuality can be relational, recreational, or both at different times. In other words they can claim the freedoms men have had, and out of which they have been hocused by propaganda about the inability of women to respond in any context except that of a total relationship, etc. etc. It's true of some women. It's also true of some men, but Byron's crack that love is a part of man's life but the whole of woman's is a normative generalization – in other words, propaganda.

This is a shock for some males. That a fully turned-on woman can have 10, 15 or 20 orgasms on end and still enjoy herself, with several partners if necessary, alarms them. The advent of the pill and the increased awareness among women of what they can achieve has led to a lot of impotence among spouses who nourished comparably neurotic images of maleness. Men who in theory always wanted to meet a nympho have sometimes been scared stiff (or flaccid) by their own wives.

We don't ourselves see this particular anxiety. It goes with a misconception of male performance, as well as of female; ignorance of the technique of managing longer intercourse; ignorance of the ways in which you can bring a woman to full orgasm without having an erection yourself; ignorance even of what a skillful woman can do with a non-erect penis – manually, orally and, if she has the gift of good muscles, vaginally. (In fact, women with full muscle control can perform best with a semi-erect partner who can relax and not resist their internal movements.) What we have to do now, having buried crew-cut, in-out male ideas of sexual prowess, is to see that women don't get re-hocused in the opposite sense and forced to assume that every one of them wants multiple orgasm, every one wants to swing, every one needs marathon sexual sessions. Some do, some don't. People are as different here as in every other respect. What matters is that they discover their thing, and find a partner sufficiently clued to permit them to make love so that it is sometimes his trip, sometimes hers, but always theirs.

This is one field where wider variety in partner experience really does help, though even here some people would rather not. Think what meals would be like if neither of you had ever tasted anyone else's cooking. And don't let harassing from the sidelines or the past stop you from finding your full and desired pattern of response. The folklore of the dangerous, insatiable woman expressed in locker-room ballads like "Eskimo Nell" will probably just not make sense to an unafraid generation who have learned what maleness and femaleness are in terms of co-operative self-realization. If we can make up for the hundreds of years spent in turning women off, men as well as women will learn to enjoy the results.

One point on which the male is emphatically the weaker sex is in the dependence of his sense of maleness on the role-playing imposed on him by society. Women have been afflicted in the same way (some get very upset, or feel defeminized, if the wife-and-mother role gives out), but we have the impression that long before Women's Lib they played the role-game less wholeheartedly than men. The role society has imposed on men has been varied by the preoccupations of the men. It has ranged from a crude and basically childish stereotype of constant erection (making for trouble when it isn't constant, merely normal), to invincibility with women (leading to rejection when women have other ideas, or put them down, intentionally, accidentally or by being smarter or more successful than they). Being responsible for your wife, stereotype-pattern, and your children is no bad thing. But we now see numerous cases of impotence and depression in unemployed males which are exacerbated, not relieved, if the wife is still earning well. One might have thought they'd be glad the family income was safe and swapped roles by mutual agreement until the business outlook improved, but no – a breadwinning woman is threatening, has stolen your testicles, and so on.

One could pursue these dangerous male support-mechanisms through a whole tradition: brawling if another man insults your woman (she's quite able to put

him down by contempt without creating an ugly scene), the mania for firearms as surrogate penises and even the terrifying threat of identical hairstyles in the two sexes. There are good Freudian reasons why men should be the more anxious sex, but a lot of the reactions they have been encouraged to form against this anxiety simply have to be unlearned if we are to have reasonable relations between males and females in a society of equal opportunities.

In a clued and affectionate couple, neither is weaker except when it comes to lifting furniture. He can't have or suckle babies, and never will be able to. She can't father them. Each has special needs derived from childhood, but these will be roughly complementary. As to achievement on the one hand and chores on the other, each will be delighted by the other's success without silly or sulking competition, and who does what when (earning, children, dishes) is settled by sensible discussion – just as who takes the initiative in bed is determined by how both feel at the time.

Couples
& Others

love

Love is the mutually satisfying sharing of each other's experience and the experience of each other – with no built-in time requirement. The use of affection to manipulate, cause guilt, invite sympathy, settle scores, produce or express dependence, or invade, annex or entrap another person is not love.

Many of the people who talk loudest about love, in its conventional meaning of making someone live up to their expectations, are neurotics incapable of loving anyone except themselves. So are the totally doormat-like who expect love to abolish any expectations of their own. The genuine article occurs between mutually respecting people, whether it's lifelong or for once only.

marriage

Over a large part of human history, marriage hasn't primarily been concerned with sex but with two other things – property and kinship, which had similar functions, because kin are a resource. Until the start of the last century property and kinship were still two of the most important motives in marriage among rich people, and finding an efficient workmate was the main concern if you were poor. During the 19th century a new emphasis appeared. More and more marriage and love were seen as a lifelong perpetuation of the peak experience of courtship, that of two individuals living wholly in and for each other, in a state of mutual self-absorption and mutual proprietorship. It's the kitsch version of this that figures in old movies and some unlib women's magazines.

In its original inspiration, this new or sentimental idea of marriage wasn't wholly retrogressive. It started to treat women as people rather than as bearer bonds, and it recognized the possibility of exploring sensibility and sensuousness. At the same time it badly sentimentalized both parenthood and expectation. Because living happily ever after was top of the menu it injected an element of intense insecurity. Warning lights started to come on if either partner's involvement became less than total 24 hours a day, or if either threatened to develop or change at all, and it took over and transferred to a psychological and emotional level all the old property considerations. In the old dispensation men were jealous of their wives as real estate or the producers of their children. Under the romantic dispensation they were permitted to stay jealous in the interests of total mutual involvement, and to lay loyalty, fidelity and so on upon them – note the financial symbolism when a wife is said to be cheating. Since the new concept was more equal, wives now asserted proprietorship of their husbands, who were part of *their* real estate – what has been neatly called penile servitude for life.

Much "romantic" love was in fact a good and rewarding interchange which could be lifelong, where these
features weren't prominent, and where the thing was an
open-ended mutual adventure. In other cases it led at
worst to mutual parasitism disguised as love and masking
a lot of hostility, or at best to affectionate relations with
both parties aware that parts of their life were like a
deposit box with two keys needed to open it, of which
each partner had only one. It wasn't realistic, however,
to talk about any sort of open-ended relationship,
tailored to different people, so long as large families were
compulsory, because fertility does impose fixity on
marriage.

The positive features of this marital style were that it
started to recognize men and women as equals capable
of a total sensual and emotional experience. The negative
features were its unsocial privacy, which overexposed
people to each other and children to adults, and its
insistence on total permanence, both in expectation and
in social convention. This brought in an element not of
security but of anxiety and proprietorship, leading to a
covert custodial relation between the parties.

We don't now have this style of marriage in America.
What we do have is often the pretence of it (which still
makes the expectation of many naive youngsters who
marry totally unrealistic) and the practice of serial polygamy helped out by adultery. The main reasons behind
this shift are threefold: greater intolerance of social
fictions and preference for telling it like it is; voluntary
fertility; and longer lives. Victorian pietists were frequently liberated from an overpossessive relationship by
the lamented death of a spouse – the lamentation dis-
charged guilt at the fact of release. With lifespans pushing
the 80s and a decline in premature deaths, until Death
do us part is now one hell of a long time. The state of
mutual sufficiency would have to continue through what
are effectively two consecutive lives, including the sharp
revaluation period (second adolescence) which most
people experience in the late 40s or early 50s when
children are grown and fantasy needs are re-evaluated
to see if there is still time to meet them.

Security is utterly necessary in a relationship between
man and woman. In youth it need only be the security
that this is the right person for now. In middle age and
after children, where two people have built a complete
life-pattern, emotional and economic, it's still needed.
Yet this is the time when for a variety of reasons it may,
and sometimes positively has to, crumble or be re-
arranged – a prospect for which traditional expectation
simply doesn't prepare people.

Marriage in Christian countries is still supposed to be

the permanent sexual union of one man and one woman to the exclusion of all others. The supposing is done not only by the Church and the State, but also by a sizeable number of people undertaking it. Others, especially among the young, would say that this isn't in fact what it does mean in modern America, and either won't go through the form because they regard advance pledges nobody can really make as dishonest, or marry with their own reservations.

It's quite true that a high proportion of modern American marriages end in divorce, that a high proportion of people have more than one spouse in a lifetime, and that few men, and only slightly more women, have sexual experience in a lifetime with only one partner. A frequent pattern is the compromise one of serial polygamy (one marriage at a time) coupled with at least some spoken or unspoken tolerance of sexual experience with other people. This adultery is often condoned on condition that it is discreet or secret and not anxiety-producing for the other partner, or that it isn't serious, that is, that it doesn't involve any competing commitment of any lasting sort.

In the general flux of experimentation at the moment it's easy to overlook the fact that even among younger people the traditional pattern not only exists but works, and that for many couples it isn't an imposition but a strong preference. Its drawbacks are the problems of the age, which we've outlined, and its outstanding advantage is that *in our culture* it seems the least harmful environment for rearing children, unless you want to experiment with them. Even authorities who think the isolated nuclear family harms children would agree that serial polygamy is about the worst system. Granted that the children of two fighting people who won't divorce may be deprived of what could be a better milieu, the many-times married couples we meet who trail around half-a-dozen kids by different people and spend odd weekends on statutory visits to others (visits they often use to perpetuate old scores) are probably laying up bad trouble for the children in their relations with the other sex and by way of general insecurity. Kids are surprisingly tough, but not all of them. The blame lies here not with serial polygamy as such but with immature adult attitudes to children and emotional self-indulgence in having them because they are cute, socially expected, or a way out of one's own inability to handle an existing relationship. Now that children are a question of either choice or negligence, it's about time we kept the word "marriage" for a life-style devoted to raising them in a stable environment, preferably not in an embattled nuclear family, but in a setup which is indissoluble until they are psychologically self-supporting.

Parenthood shouldn't be undertaken unless you are willing and able to finish the job.

Marriage also has contractual advantages in that it regularizes the business side of the relations between two people who live together. But for adults whose bond is companionate and sexual, "primary relationship" is a much better phrase: it bypasses the law books, implies commitment, but is unrigid in that it is for the parties to decide what exactly that means for them. Primary relationships can change, sometimes coexist, and supplement each other. Using another name doesn't draw the teeth of human living, prevent sorrow and rejection, or stop people fighting, but it tends to the recognition that love is a relation not a romance or a margarine commercial. It also humanizes secondary relationships by insisting that they are relationships, not intrigues (in which the third party gets exploited and deserves it), nor threatening and shabby conspiracies against the other member of the primary pair. It recognizes the true facts: that while in a good couple each is largely sufficient unto the other, no two people are wholly so, nor do they own each other. At the same time one primary relationship is as much as most people want, need, or can handle. Conventional marriage modernized by depriving it of the concept of mutually jealous ownership does suit many couples even if they don't have children. What it fails to recognize institutionally is the wide variety of human needs, which include total couple-involvement but aren't confined to it. The idea that no pattern of relationship or behavior, conventional or otherwise, suits everybody is the most important one we have to get across, whether that be monogamy, heterosexuality, liberated womanhood, conventional womanhood, swinging, being a celibate monk or anything else whatsoever.

Since society is more or less bound to institutionalize relationships, it will ultimately recognize this variety in law by matching up responsibilities with obligations and dropping essentially religious differences between wives and mistresses, legitimate and illegitimate children. At present it talks monogamy but accepts serial polygamy – an instance of Herman Kahn's idea that a bit of hypocrisy tends to keep up standards. It would be better occupied in localizing marriage in the cradle, not the vagina, but that may be too much to hope for.

Open marriage, as it now figures in the literature, really represents the kind of compromise which humane folk would naturally accept in living together – in particular getting rid of sex-role nonsenses, both those imposed traditionally on the man and those which make the woman an inferior partner. The traditional man-woman roles may have been appropriate once, and were at least accepted. Basically the woman, in exchange for being obedient, chaste and excluded from male occupations, acquired a permanent right to the custodial proprietorship of the man, while he, in exchange for giving her economic security, got custodial rights over her virtue. This kind of thing is just no longer relevant to real people. Members of an open marriage are equals, support each other, divide what has to be done between them, discuss and resolve fairly the competing claims of their separate ambitions and wishes, avoid hurting or rejecting each other but don't rely on blackmail to keep property rights in one another. They are loving and committed but not jealous, and try to build security on adult instead of neurotic attitudes. That would be a fair rule-book for most sexual primary relationships, and a lot more realistic than the conventional idea of female obedience plus penile servitude for life.

mischief-makers

Avoid them. They can be especially bad news in a threesome, but you can get mischief-making couples who cause disruption wherever they go. A group usually comes to cope with them or throws them out, but they can cause a lot of harm before this happens.

We're talking about specifically sexual mischief-makers, who get satisfaction from invading and upsetting a primary relationship, not the ordinary kind – stupid relatives and neighbors, spying landlords and so on. The latter are commonly recognizable, while the sexual sort often look like friendly swingers, but tend to move in, seduce people rather than relate to them, and their own relationship to each other is that of accomplices, not lovers. There's a classic portrait of a mischief-making duo in *Les Liaisons Dangereuses*. Anyone who doesn't actively increase your couple-closeness is a bad choice for a threesome or a foursome, and make sure you yourselves don't act disruptively or intrusively with couples to whom you relate. Reinforcement is a matter of extreme tact in reading and giving nonverbal cues. Non-sharing couples can also be exposed to mischief-making, but most of this is verbal: a couple who aren't jealous aren't easily split up by tattle.

It's wise to keep clear of disturbing people, generally – judging them by the views they express. They're often as mean and vicious in their private as in their public life.

othello and all that

Jealousy, in its theater and opera sense, isn't natural, built-in, mammalian or the like. It's a social convention which people have been taught is an index of love and marital propriety.

Fear of rejection, losing a love object, being put down, outclassed or supplanted by someone else, is natural, built-in and human. It follows from this, if you think about it, that secure and communicating couples who include each other in all their fantasies and pleasures aren't jealous.

The operatic attitude goes on causing suffering. If the person you marry is highly skilled and highly attractive you might expect that others would wish to enjoy sex with him or her sometimes, and since sex isn't an asset which wastes with use, one possible reaction to this would be to feel chuffed at the compliment to your luck and judgment. The response prescribed by society, however, is that you ought to behave like a backward five-year-old who sees another child with his tricycle – and also break off the love relationship or keep it going as part of a heavy guilt and forgiveness scene. This looks idiotic and is. Love is a giving relationship, yet in our tradition the hallmark of togetherness is that you acquire unlimited rights to block the loved one's fantasies. This is topsy-turvy.

Huge tracts of European literature have been built

on this series of extraordinary conventions. The next generation may find it about as reasonable as the ritual guilt of Orestes, but the lobster quadrille ("did they?" "will she?" "with whom?" "does she know?") goes on pathetically in middle-class society.

The trouble is that we have been encouraged to confuse fear of rejection (real) with jealousy (conventional). Now that parenthood is controllable the only original basis for hardline male jealousy is obsolete. Fidelity doesn't mean today that nothing goes on below the waist, it means real couple confidence and couple unity and not doing dangerous, rejecting, or anxiety-producing things. Sex with others (taking care also that the others concerned won't be hurt or upset by it) may or may not be involved – for some couples fidelity is really total complementarity so that the idea of any third parties turns them off. If any outside sex happens, it must include, not exclude, your primary partner – by full communication if not by participation – and the motive for avoiding a particular situation will be concern, not a species of male or female chauvinist copyright convention. Loving people are lovers not jailers to each other. They grant one another's fantasies, enjoy one another's pleasures, and speak up at once if something that either is doing

threatens, upsets, or puts them down. On this basis they can live as free but mutually concerned people, sensitive to what it is and isn't safe to do.

This is some way from strangling (or divorcing) a beautiful woman whom you love, and who loves you, because you think she may have slept once with Cassio. Nobody would blame Othello – he came from a jealous culture, felt put down by whites because he was black, and had his ear poisoned about her fooling him. In that frame of mind he'd hardly be inclined to speculate that maybe she'd like to try it with someone uncircumcised and ask her how she had liked it. As we come to separate jealousy of the conventional kind from rejection-feelings, we may get more, not less, sympathy for Othello. Rejection is one of the worst things that afflicts us, and openness in marriage, not conventional jealousy, is the way to see it doesn't happen to us.

relational, recreational

Sex in humans has three functions. It can be reproductive (producing babies), relational (expressing love and bonding adults together), or recreational (play and fun). Most human problems over sex arise from anxiety over, and confusion among, these modes.

If human sex were "ordained for the procreation of children," we shouldn't mate all the year round and throughout pregnancy, but one or two times a year (as some rather cracked theologians would have us do). Until recently religion, which in our culture traditionally rejects pleasure as a motive, actually taught that reproduction was the only decent use of sexuality. With the growth of the romantic idea of marriage it shifted its ground, rather behind the event, so that today, together with crypto-religious psychiatry and counseling, it asserts that worthy sex can only be relational.

There has been no time in human history when either of these valuations was wholly true, though they have served to bolster up the uses to which the family has been subjected. Even in very kin-minded cultures gaps were left for sexual activity which wasn't an expression either of the wish for children or all-embracing personal closeness. Normally these gaps were provided for males only: they were the legislators and claimed the right to nonrelational sex, while prohibiting their women from doing so by means of moral codes, purdah or, more subtly, the indoctrination of girls with the notion that relational sex is the sole kind of which women are capable, and that unlike men they can't enjoy unless they possess totally. (Recreationally-minded women were obviously needed as well to make this ploy work, but they were outside good society. The whole system back-

fired badly, however, because a large number of men were impotent with "respectable" wives since sex was now something you didn't do to a nice girl.)

The pill has totally altered this. Safe from compulsory pregnancy, many women have now discovered that their capacity to experience sex at all three levels, either together or on different occasions and in different contexts, is as great as any man's if not greater. The adult of today has all three options – sex for parenthood, sex as total relationship, and sex for fun accompanied by no more than affection. Older folks looking at the young today realize how much their generation suffered through society's scheming to confuse these modes – when play between boy and girl led to forced marriage between acquaintances, or when one partner misread the other's mind or simulated love and concern to get a relation-minded partner into bed.

All good sex is partly relational. If it's really good it generates a relationship, even if only of warmth and gratitude, and nobody wants sex even at the play-level with a person who isn't considerate and caring. At the same time it can perfectly well express anything from total involvement to a romp between friends. The important thing is that all these are worthy aspects of human interaction provided the partners fully share their estimate of the level of concern involved. Sex may, through its intensely reinforced bonding ability, change two people who engage in it and make them closer: it can, that is, be an open-ended experience. Accordingly you have to pattern your choices by common sense and you have a responsibility to avoid upsetting vulnerable people. There are some people you wouldn't take mountaineering. For robust folk of high self-esteem, recreational sex with tenderness is good. For couples, it is best incorporated into the couple relationship so that recreational relationships involve and include them both, instead of leaving one out. Don't above all, misread recreational as frivolous or exploitative. It means playful, caring and tender.

sandstone

Name of an estate in Topanga, California, which was the site of an extended experiment in open sexuality. It figures in all informed discussion of the subject because so far it is the only such experiment to be completely frank about its intentions. It illustrates so many of our points that it merits discussion at length.

California abounds in encounter and sensitivity centers. People who go there do or don't find themselves, whatever that means (reassessing their goals and finding out what they really want is the most usual meaning), but a high proportion have the air of going through a lot of psycho-makework and verbal behaviors when the real object of the exercise is to get laid. At Sandstone, one could quite frankly go to get laid – but with that out of the way, participants were surprised to find that sensitivity, encounter and a good deal of genuine self-education quite often followed. They both enjoyed themselves and did reassess their goals and self-image. Sandstone was many straight people's first and only encounter with genuinely open sexuality in a structured setting, and the fact that it recreated an intense experience of infantile innocence in hung-up adults makes many who went there nostalgic or overenthusiastic about it. But allowing for this its capacity to facilitate the sort of growth at which individual psychology aims was pretty remarkable.

Sandstone was a large sierra estate with a ranch-type house and a covered, hot pool. In the house, the upper large room had a fireplace, sun balcony and ordinary furnishings. The downstairs was an enormous room with a small one adjoining, both with red shag carpets, low lights and mattresses.

A small group of people ("the family") lived in and maintained the estate, and others who came were effectively John and Barbara Williamson's guests. Intending members might visit once, but then had to join if they wanted to come again, at a tab of $250 per year. Only couples were admitted – a single visitor had to bring a partner.

On several nights a week there was open house for the 400 or so couples who were members. On some of these occasions visitors brought their own food, but on Saturdays an excellent, buffet-style dinner was provided, and visitors might stay overnight. The pattern on Wednesdays was similar but the numbers (often as many as 50 on a Saturday) much smaller. Sunbathing and the hot pool were always available. Nudity was general, but neither that nor anything else except ordinarily civilized behavior was obligatory – a structure without rules was maintained by the general mores of the group. Open sexual expression of any kind was allowed anywhere (except on the front lawn, after a police helicopter nearly crashed while observing it). Drugs and minors were banned, and alcohol not greatly encouraged.

Description, especially to people doubtful about any kind of open sex experience, fails signally to convey what Sandstone did or why. The essential point is that in spite of enthusiastic sex on all sides it was wholly unlike a brothel, and wholly like a relaxed home, the keynote not being excitement or lasciviousness but innocence, once the freakout produced in strangers by its openness was over. A party consisted of a shared meal, a lot of conversation, and a gradual drift downstairs for those who chose to go, others staying upstairs talking, reading, or singing with a guitar. No expectation was laid on anyone – hardline swingers would rush downstairs to start scoring, more timid newcomers would put a head into the "ballroom" and retreat: many if not most people stayed with regular partners or in a group with their friends. A typical figure was the woman whose husband was downstairs, with her permission, but who did not want to go down herself in case she was approached by someone she did not fancy. Sitting upstairs talking to the family she would eventually be encouraged to go down and join him – and learn to say no when she meant it. Any attempt at hassling by an overeager male would be interrupted by other members, for men had to learn that no is a preference not a putdown. There were a few bad trips through being left out, but these would be cured by learning that all things usually came to him or her who waited.

Homosexual contacts between men were rare (to the regret of some women, who would have liked to watch two men together) but common between women. Black people were represented on the membership file in roughly the same proportion as in Los Angeles. Some stayed together, as with other couples, some not. Nobody – except an unusually attractive woman or man – was strongly encouraged to join in, and nobody played host or hostess to shy newcomers. It was thought better to let them watch, learn the rules, and become gradually open to the experience. Actual sex-play tended to be conventional – idiosyncratic fantasy was a little inhibited by the group scene.

The commonest story among couples who found Sandstone a good trip and, in Dr. Ralph Yaney's words, "the finishing school for psychoanalysis," was this: they would come once, not undress, watch, wonder if they approved, decide they didn't, and leave. About a month later they would be back, and keep coming. On the first few occasions they would stay strictly together, being stimulated by watching other couples, and enjoying the company. Ultimately the jealousy barrier would yield – often by way of a threesome – and there would be an upsurge of relief and closeness. Others, more aggressive, would start determined to swing, the man bringing the girl by the hair because it would do her good. When 15 minutes after going downstairs she was fully turned on to both sexes and he hadn't made it yet with anyone, he would panic and suggest they leave: she would reply "no way," and there would be a row down the parking lot. This pattern involved a fair amount of a high-speed education for the man with regard to the relative sexual appetites and capacities of the sexes.

In the "ballroom" every occasion was different. Sometimes with too many people, it was like Grand Central
Station and any atmosphere of relaxation was lost. At
other times, and especially on Wednesdays when the
company was smaller, it could be totally relaxed, charismatic, tender or zanily playful like the varying moods of
a single, very good couple – but still in the group. On
Sunday mornings early wakers would go up and make

coffee, to be followed by a handful of first-timers trying to work out what had hit them and needing to talk about it, then by the rest of the party. Breakfast often ended as an impromptu seminar on something. (Sandstone members were united only by being a high IQ group of achievers, drawn heavily from the professions.) Some of these morning-after experiences were even more rewarding than the specifically sexual part of Sandstone, and certainly complementary to it.

A lot of our notes on the psychology and advisability

or otherwise of open sexual experiences are based on observation of this single experiment. There are others – involving different income groups or different ideologies – some successful, others positively harmful, but this was in our view the best structured.

The idea of a wholly open sexual scene is so fantasy-loaded, out of our culture, and generally mindblowing that it's difficult, short of the experience, to assess how one would react to it and what its effects would be. Apart from reactions like "Wow!" or "Disgusting!" men tended to be stimulated by the idea but apprehensive that they would fail to perform, women to be stimulated but apprehensive that the experience would be danger-ous or distasteful, and in particular that they would find themselves under pressure to have sex with males they didn't fancy. Couples were apprehensive that they would react with jealousy and find the involvement disruptive. Rather than finding these fears justified, most couples described their experience as one of "release."

The main components in this release were probably relief of simple acceptability and performance anxieties in a scene where everyone is acceptable and nobody has to perform; relief from socially-imposed role-playing and the general shift of sexuality in all its aspects from "hot" (excited, anxious) to "cool" (gentle, permitted); the revival of playfulness, childishness and personhood in the group.

It's not obvious why having sex in company should have so big a beneficial effect on some people, a question which is bound to be asked by a culture brought up on privacy. That in fact may well be the reason – privacy means that we experience others as hostile to our sexuality. Either they would disapprove and punish it, or they're Peeping Toms, or they would try to take our partner away. To drop privacy, stop checking if there's a crack in the shades, and experience others outside our sexual relation as approving, enjoying, encouraging, even applauding, and only joining in to reinforce, not threaten, our primary relationship can well be encountered by some people as a total reversal of attitudes they've learned to their hurt. Most of us have learned such atti-tudes, even if we rationalize them by saying that love is a secret and private thing which would be devalued if other people saw it – which is another way of saying that it would be threatened or disapproved of.

Another beneficial fact related to this was that low-dominance people of both sexes came to take their cues from the more dominant and actively learn self-esteem in a sexual context. One can alter attitudes by altering behaviors, as well as the other way around. Timid men who learned to address women because they saw others do so, timid women who learned by watching that other people actively enjoyed things which scared them, certainly found that the psychodrama and performance element in changing their behaviors under the group influence heightened their confidence and self-esteem. Stereotypes about age or ugliness tended to be punctured – nearly everyone was desirable and demonstrably desired, the exceptions being those who were avoided because of their behaviors (and learned to change them or left). In a society hung up on thinness, fat men and women scored as often as thin ones, and newcomers could see this.

Most important for couples was the exorcism of all the custodial anxieties of conventional marriage. In shared openness, as opposed to closed swinging, which is anxiety-promoting, at least until the couple has compared notes after (see *Swinging*), both sexes found that the sight of a lover relating sexually to someone else – often while still holding their regular partner's hand – was moving, exciting and finally immensely releasing. There was nothing to be afraid of. Afterward they were often more tender to each other because of a feeling that the parts of their personhood which they felt had been taken had been returned as a loving gift. This may sound like a sentimental apology for an outbreak of animal spirits, but isn't – a good group experience is charismatic rather than lascivious, cool rather than horny, and much more like religion than sex in anthropological terms. Some of these unobvious and unexpected responses answer the question "If they've got good sex already, why do they need it?"

Other unconscious elements are probably important too – the tribal feeling (it would be interesting to know if deprived children or only children got more out of it) and the stirrings of a reconciliation with normal bisexuality. All that can be said is that the Sandstone experience was a very powerful, rather complex, and apparently for the people then involved a non-dangerous tool by which for a variety of reasons they were enabled to get in touch with feelings and needs they had neglected.

It ought to be obvious that not everyone is going to benefit from this or any other similar experience, and that there are those who are going to be upset by it – as some people are gravely upset by, say, religious conversion or childbirth. Coming out of convention into the cold looks risky, and counselors wouldn't (rightly) hurry to recommend it if you don't know your own mind. There are obvious hazards apart from the risk you may outrun or upset yourself (which goes for any powerful new experience). Couples who have been rubbing along, more or less, may find that experiences which make one

or both of them change can end the relationship. But this is equally true of psychotherapy or a new job, and sometimes outgrowing a relationship is obligatory. Any group sex scene involves some risk of VD, though Sandstone was lucky over this. (For future experiments, it is important that the participants be responsible people and not generally promiscuous.) The main hazard is that the Sandstone mix, of people, milieu and structure, isn't going necessarily to be recreated elsewhere. With the wrong people going about it the wrong way, and all starting with the anxieties and the "hot" sex attitude normal to most of us, private swing parties can be bad trips. Accordingly, if you decide to try to reproduce the experiences we've described, make sure you go about it the right way.

A final less obvious complication is addiction. People who went to Sandstone regularly seemed to be of several kinds. Some came very frequently at first, worked through some kind of experience, and thereafter came back at intervals to top up their relationship, swelling the nucleus of "cool" regulars who enjoyed the sun, the sex and the company as a relaxation – rather like regulars at a nudist club, but with sex added. Often this pattern was determined by where they lived and how far they had to come – they treated the group as a second home. A few were hard swingers who came solely to see how often they could score in an evening. For them, the scene was a kind of athletic relaxation – perfectly worthy, but one wouldn't have needed them in a majority. Some came, passed through a substantial inner experience, didn't need more, and left or dropped out. All these seemed to be getting positive benefit. A few came when very vulnerable, swung wildly with everyone, were disgusted with themselves and quit, wishing they hadn't been. Others were there all of the time possible and appeared to be using the group scene as a refuge from active involvement in life. They resembled the wife-swapping swingers who end up knowing nobody but swingers and talking about nothing else – rather as with some chess- and bridge-players' activities which start as games and end as social disabilities. This is what we mean by addiction. If sex gets to be a substitute for life, you've got problems which need dealing with.

seriousness

Seriousness about sex differs vastly from person to person. "Some take it like the Host, some like a toffee," and there are Quixotes and Sanchos. In Strauss's *Ariadne auf Naxos*, when Ariadne, who lives at the high-tragic level, is deserted by a Hero, she can be consoled finally only by a God. For her maid, the soubrette, it's simply a case of off with the old love, on with the new.

Our culture has probably greatly overvalued intensity. Some people can't help it – it is natural and proper to them – but there's no virtue and some harm in over-cultivating it, and some virtue and no harm in tender playfulness. Tragic intensities tend to produce bad trips, not peak experiences.

sharing

Sharing means exactly what it says – the sharing of sexual experience with another couple (not "swapping" which is something quite different). Some lovers find this an invasion of their privacy: others find it a resource. The essence of sharing is that two couples make love in each other's presence; no more than that. See *Watching, Massage, Threesomes*.

A couple who both wish to try it (and "both" excludes going along with a partner out of loyalty or for peace and quiet), should start by putting out of their heads anything they have read about orgies, wife-swapping and the like.

Most of these are masturbatory fantasies. Next, they should forget about sexual excitement as the aim of the experience. Sex in a group scene can be exciting, but the main experience in sharing is quietude, and the intention is sensual rather than sexual. The experience of sharing we're talking about quite often involves no cross-couple contacts more sexual than touch. A sharing occasion can go on to complete sexual involvement of all the parties, but most often it doesn't. Its value doesn't depend on doing so, and the participants should be at liberty to impose any restraints which accord with their own feelings and reservations. This won't spoil the experience; if it is going too far or too fast, they can turn it aside into simple sharing of intimacy.

The fundamental consideration for everyone is to be careful when choosing the couple or couples to share with. Self-advertised swingers are the worst people, as they will try to hurry on to a sexual exchange. Best friends aren't a good choice either, unless it happens naturally. The ideal is a couple both of whom both partners like and who aren't in the throes of a marital problem. If the

choice is wise none of the participants should find subsequent social intercourse embarrassing or overintense.

Usually the evening starts with a group meal – a good beginning to any religious experience, which is what this becomes if it works. Drink shouldn't be used as a disinhibitor, wine with the meal is plenty. Then the lights are turned down and the couples relax together, not in chairs,

sitting-room fashion, but in a dream setting, on mattresses, in front of a fire if it's cold, and side by side.

At an early stage, they introduce shared nakedness.
This can be done by swimming, sunbathing, or hot
tubbing (q.v.) before the meal, or each partner can undress the other in front of the fire. Once undressed,
everyone relaxes completely and talks. If it seems natural,
they start to make love of the gentlest kind to their own
partner – massage, touch, kisses. Sometimes they go on
to intercourse if and when it seems right and natural. If it
doesn't, they shouldn't. The other couple will probably

follow; if not, no one should be disappointed – but go back to quiet enjoyment of each other's company. Making love in warm company isn't lascivious or embarrassing but often movingly innocent. Don't at any price give an exhibition – it would be insensitive.

Afterward is the time for some extended pillow talk (playing tapes or records all the time spoils this). In the right company the couples feel a deep relaxation even greater than after making love alone. If things are so arranged that there are pillows and blankets, they can sleep and breakfast together. Next morning is often the best part.

This simple sharing is more often than not a safe and beneficial sexual and sensual experience for any two normal couples all of whose members want it. It's neither embarrassing nor disturbing, and if it's unpleasant or unrewarding they picked the wrong couple. Quite obviously, however, the potential is there for such an experience to go on perfectly naturally to express the sensual (not necessarily sexual) involvement between them. Girls being loved side by side often hold hands. A couple sitting close to a lovemaking couple (and they should be close, not on opposite sides of the room) can become involved in touching, massaging and being touched. If this happens they need both to feel that all of them are securely in control of the situation (so that they can quite gently put a hand aside if they don't want it there – no isn't a putdown), and at the same time not block the growth of the experience. Sometimes the two girls embrace, then invite the men in. But the pace isn't horny or excited, more like that of mutual sensual massage. Some couples go the whole way to full sexual involvement of all four people, but this is neither necessary nor integral to the experience unless they wish it to be. When it does happen, it may overcome anxieties about their partners as a source of rejection threats and prohibitions. The slowest member of the foursome sets the pace. If one person doesn't want to be more involved, the others should cool it back to touching and resting, or simple massage.

There is no scenario for sharing. It is ruined by expectation, or attempts to stage-manage, seduce or push. Taken at this level of cool and control, there is no reason why any normally robust couple should find it harmful to their relationship, provided neither of them was positively turned off by the idea and pressured into trying it. (Being doubtful isn't the same thing, for doubt can be relieved when they see that the experience isn't turning out to be what they thought.)

Sharing can help rather than harm people with sexual (not marital) problems, but a couple should not go into business as amateur therapists, or persuade people to share, even at the least sexual level, because they think it would do them good. With the right people, and even without any intense sexual involvement, it can be a charismatic experience, but it's only for couples who communicate fully, know their minds, and are willing to follow their feelings in saying yes or no. The really important thing, especially where the interchange does become sexual, is that the couples act as couples and reinforce each other's couple bond. If one person sits there hating it while the other three make furious love, it's a bad and destructive scene.

Some couples who are used to full sexual exchange jump in without preliminaries. Others shouldn't be misled by this into missing the sensual education which makes them able to relate like this: the result is the ordinary sort of swing party, which isn't sharing. When a couple shares regularly at any level they can invite another couple to join them, but they must not forget that the newcomers have the anxieties they had and need the full, gradual experience – let them simply watch if they prefer. Lastly, no one should start a big group or a club unless they are willing to elder them and act as permission-givers. They inevitably run into disturbed and disturbing people, would-be studs who won't let their women take part, and VD problems. Equally, a couple should avoid creating expectation, giving a sex party, or souring the atmosphere of innocence and relaxation – though if sharing has worked for them, they won't want to.

swinging

In primitive societies – or what we call primitive, meaning societies that are technically simple but emotionally sophisticated – people exchange wives and husbands under fairly strict conditions. Lending a (willing) wife may be a gesture of hospitality, but it's a convenient one. Like any other favor it imposes obligation, and because this favor is sexual it increases the number of your kin – he borrowed your wife, so you can borrow his canoe or his help in hunting. Orgies (meaning no-taboos, no-holds-barred sexual fiestas) occur on set occasions, often against a background of strict propriety at other times. They counteract the repressive and disruptive effect of hard-line morals, make all the participants children again for one limited occasion, and perhaps boost the general fertility of the crops (if crops were moralistic they might not grow). Everyone comes out of these occasions breathless, guiltless, and ready to return to propriety. Easy-going people who treat sex as a gentle sport also hold what look to us like orgies, but these are just the relaxed enjoyment in company of what they already enjoy in private – as Devereux said of the Samoans, it's the equivalent of football, the movies and the Saturday night binge.

Our society – technically advanced and emotionally naive – doesn't think in this way. If in America and in other countries increasing numbers of married couples are getting courage from media accounts of swinging to try to develop rituals that involve others in their sexuality without sacrificing the primary relationship, overwhelmingly the biggest motives are greater emancipation (leading to impatience with the proprietary idea of marriage as mutual ownership) and sexual restlessness. Another is probably that which inspires wife-swapping Eskimos, namely shortage of kin. The double standard seems to us merely disgusting, and the conventional American solution of serial polygamy with adultery (see *Marriage*) merely dishonest. Accordingly, the search to fulfill the need for experience outside the couple can represent honesty and mutual concern rather than lust – when it works, that is, and when it is reciprocal.

In a culture still overtly disapproving, swingers, like nudists, represent a charismatic subculture with a shared turnon and a shared secret. They seek out other like-minded couples, sometimes sight unseen on the strength of advertisements, and exchange with them on a no-commitment basis. Since so many kinds of people are involved it is difficult to assess how much they get from it, how far women or men are dragged in to avoid losing a spouse, and the relative proportions of those who find that swinging rejuvenates their marriage and those who have thoroughly bad trips. Psychologists are equally split between those with participant experience, who tend

to be favorable, and those without, who are denunciatory or apprehensive. The few impartial studies are downbeat in assessing ultimate results. Swingers may discharge fears and fantasies to their benefit, feel closer because their spouses are seen as giving them back their freedom, and – more rarely – acquire genuine surrogate kin. Others retain all their prejudices intact, and simply add swinging to a rather limiting life-style as they might add golf, sometimes with equally divisive effects.

Swinging may be "closed" (the couples exchange, but have sex in separate rooms) or "open," leading to a foursome. On the basis of our observations we would expect the consequences of these two modes to be quite different. In a foursome all the participants observe what occurs and can discharge anxieties by learning, while the element of normal bisexuality which our culture represses and which underlies all mate-exchange in primates has a chance to surface (which may be why conventional swingers – and there are plenty of them – are scared of foursomes). Male pressure still leads to some very bad trips – women are less inclined to accept random partners, and the system of long-range dating by advertisements or pick-up joints almost guarantees them.

That a sizable minority still finds swinging immensely rewarding is good anthropological evidence that there is something there, but it seems the wrong, or not the best, initial way to go about the search for that something, except for very robust and secure people. Sharing sex is a powerful experience and by ritualizing it with virtual strangers one is unable to tap some of its power – notably to transfer sex and its anxieties from the "hot" category prescribed by an irritated culture to the "cool" category based on nonanxiety, noncompulsion and recognition of personhood.

It is beneficial to realize that in some sexual contexts we and our partners temporarily become unpersons (in making no socially prescribed demands), but it is also limiting to ritualize this too much.

We're not saying "don't" to couples attracted to swinging experiments by their needs and after full discussion. But we do suggest they read what we've said about other types of generalized sexual experience and try to work out how, if at all, to go about it. Swapping with strangers is a bad start, and swapping with close friends can be divisive unless it happens absolutely naturally, and sometimes even then. The most rewarding experiences, if you aren't too obsessed with scoring, are those with people who can relax with you until anything that happens happens naturally and nobody is disappointed if nothing does.

threesomes

A threesome involving a permanent couple and a third party can be a uniquely moving sexual experience if the conditions are right (and a complete turnoff if they are wrong). It also represents by far the commonest first experience of extended sexuality.

The third member can be of either sex. The two like-sex participants, instead of experiencing the jealousy expected by society, often become extremely close even though nobody has any sex at all – a kind of sisterhood or brotherhood. In the case of women this can lead to quite unexpected mutual sex-expression that has nothing lesbian about it, and may greatly excite the man. They shouldn't be upset afterward if this has happened – it's wholly normal. Most men stay at the level of strong

friendship, but may go further if the idea of male contacts doesn't disturb them – usually they treat the woman
as a bridge between them.

A threesome will not work if one partner imports a
lover whose aims are intrusive; if a couple mischievously
seduce a third party who can be thoroughly upset by
the experience, or try to use the occasion to spite the
other or prove something ("you don't know how to make
love – you should see me with Mabel"). Equally, it won't
work if they try to fuel it with gin against everyone's
better judgment. This ends with disgust and recrimina-
tions. It can work when a thoroughly secure and loving
couple who already have good sex mutually invite someone they both like, and about whom they know enough
to be sure that it is safe for all three. The relationship is a
rather subtle, two-way gift – the woman who invites
another that her man fancies is giving him a present (not
least the feeling that she is totally secure and doesn't
need to be jealous), and both are giving the third party
the gift of sharing their secure intimacy – and their sexual
knowhow. The same applies when the man does the
same for his woman.

People who are on frank terms, say "We're going to
make love, would you care to join us?" It's better to be
forthright than to try to set someone up. A threesome
starts best by gentle proximity, with the odd-sex partner
in the middle. The couple then both pay attention to the
guest (massage is a great start, unembarrassing between
males, which can gradually become sexual). Sometimes
gentle intimacy all night with mutual intercourse seems
the right sequel – or it can get wildly playful. We heard of
a man being tossed for by the two girls – the wife won and
had the orgasm of her life. Sensible people don't program
this or any other sex experience, however. If it goes wrong,
they have the sense to stop, at the request of any of the
three players, and switch to simple intimacy – sleep or
listening to records.

Threesomes are best if both invite the newcomer as a
couple, show some sense whom they invite, play fair –
no phoney invitations and big martinis – and aren't in the
least disappointed if nothing happens.

A permanent threesome (*ménage à trois*) is obviously a totally different situation. It can and does work for
some people, but only when the three individuals involved
all relate to one another. Often they may do so for rather
special reasons: one or more of them may be strongly
bisexual; an older woman, especially if childless, may
treat a younger one with children as a sister or daughter;
two men may have a David-and-Jonathan relationship,
sexualized or not, in which they reinforce each other.
The situation is unconventional for our society but not

for Man – sororal polygamy (marrying two or more sisters simultaneously, like Jacob) is a widespread human pattern. It tends to be "economic," based on convenience in managing work and child-rearing, while fraternal polyandry (marrying several brothers, like Draupadi in the *Mahabharata*) has to do with male comradeship and bonding. Neither necessarily goes with a particular view of sex roles, and doubtless people who adopt it now would make it fill other needs. One can enumerate the kind of stresses it might lead to, especially if one of the parties was only grudgingly willing to accept the pattern. Whether these are greater than the stresses of a one-to-one relationship would depend on the people concerned.

Pair-mating animals seem to have found the same thing. Threesomes either way are fairly common in normally monogamous birds, and apparently just happen (without any deep Freudian needs on the part of the birds). Infants can bond same-sex adults – a cat whose kittens have died will take turns minding and rearing another cat's litter. Usually where two males share a mate, it is because such sharing makes them allies, not rivals, as society seems to expect, and able between them to outthreaten any third party. This could go for us, too.

Resources

behavior therapy

Nearly all human behavior is learned. It can accordingly be unlearned by training, and it is to this that behavior therapy addresses itself. Classical behaviorism (which is a psychiatric ideology, though that doesn't impair its results) is sceptical about things like emotions, feelings and drives – after all, we can only observe these if they give rise to behaviors. In rejecting "mentalism," old-style behaviorism assumes that states of mind are at least as much a result of behavior patterns as they are causes, and sets out to change the behavior. All normal people are scared in a battle. If by training you alter their behaviors, not only so that they don't run away, but so that they don't go pale, sweat, have dilated pupils and a raised heart rate, then according to the theory you've abolished fear. In fact you can alter their behaviors in this way, but through the fear of being afraid they commonly get obstinate nightmares later and need to be allowed to experience the emotion of fear, by reliving, in order to lose them.

This instance indicates the uses and limits of behavior modification by learning, though sometimes the classical theory works better than this. If you teach a downtrodden person to show dominant behaviors, his self-esteem rises through response from his fellows. Much that has been written is merely oversimple – if you reward a dog each time it raises its head above a line you can rapidly train it to jump (on the basis that rewarded behaviors tend to be repeated). However, in the course of this process there comes a time when the dog quite obviously latches on to what the experimenter wants and does it – a cat doesn't. Dogs and dolphins, but not cats, are social animals and programed to be sensitive to approval and disapproval. So are we.

We aren't, however, concerned here with theory, but with the fact that behavior therapy is uniquely good at tackling handicapping sexual behaviors and teaching new skills. It works on the assumption that behaviors which are followed by unpleasant results are less often repeated, and – much more important – that behaviors which are even nominally rewarded are reinforced and more often repeated. Society has for centuries tried to turn off unpopular forms of behavior by aversion (punishment) without much success, because they usually managed to reinforce not being found out. People changed their verbal behaviors but not their tastes. A few eager beavers have tried to treat homosexual people by aversion – involving such things as a mild shock accompanying a same-sex picture, and even tapes of mockery and abuse (a great idea, in dealing with a behavior which may reflect low dominance). Amazingly, they have been surprised at their low success rate in anything but making the subjects stop admitting to being gay. The Inquisition got similar results with redhot irons, which are a stronger aversive stimulus. The fact of setting out to treat a normal component of human response tells you something about the motivation of these quite humanely-intended studies. One sportsman tried to cure a masochist by aversion, and found to his astonishment that the patient rather liked it.

Punishment as a training method is as old as man. Far more important is the idea that where possible you should operate by reinforcing a wanted behavior by reward, not trying to turn off a complicated behavior you don't want. Aversion has its uses, but only when you've analyzed the pattern you are dealing with, and it usually calls for building up an alternative. You can avert an alcoholic from whisky and from going to the cupboard to get it (by trying to associate it in his mind with nausea), but you usually need to build up his dominance so he doesn't require it and can refuse it in company. If somebody's homosexual orientation is a bad trip and bothers him (not society – it's none of society's business), you can reinforce his heterosexual skills.

Some people have behaviors which bother both them and society – exhibitionists or child molesters. One can argue philosophically that no normal female should be upset by a normal set of genitalia, and that much of the harm to molested children (who may have been surprisingly and precociously seductive themselves) is in the consequent panic and uproar. At the same time, people are incarcerated for these things. You can help them turn off the behaviors, but a more productive attitude is to be less bothered by society's fears than the subject's problems. You set about reinforcing the normal sexual approach to adult women which they lack.

Behavior therapy using the whole range of methods is excellent at turning off unproductive hangup behaviors, turning on new sociosexual skills, getting rid of destructive behaviors like smoking, alcoholism and overeating, and helping people overcome irrational fears – of flying, of dogs, of particular situations. It's particularly good with what are called functionally autonomous habits, like impotence or frigidity. The psychoanalytic view of these, and of hangups generally, is that they represent persisting infantile anxieties – surface the anxiety and you should lose the hangup. Unfortunately this rarely works – a habit once set needs to be unlearned, or it persists long after the cause which started it. While psychoanalysis aims to improve sex by giving insight, behavior therapists realize that if you improve performance, a lot of the feedback-generated consequences of the problem go, and the subject is better able to get wise to him or herself. Naturally it can't make someone over from scratch. If the old problems are still alive they may cause new symptoms, and some patients would benefit from another form of psychotherapy as well. But at least they've lost the presenting problem. People who go to an analyst may get much information about themselves – and stay impotent or frigid.

The technique with frigidity is basically a retraining

of the body in sensuality – learning to relax, learning to masturbate, first alone, then with the other partner, and a gradual carry-over into regular sex. This progression does actually alter the person from tense and denying to relaxed and accepting. The treatment of impotence depends on the fact that we can control and condition not only behaviors we can see, but also involuntary ones like blood pressure or bowel movements, provided we can monitor them. If we're yogis we may get this knack from ten years of meditation. For others it's quicker to use some sort of display system. The impotent man has a strain gauge or a volume recorder put on his penis. He is told not to think about sex but to concentrate on moving the needle. Many men can thus acquire something which doesn't normally exist, namely the ability to produce erection at will. Since most impotent men have been anxiously willing an erection in a way that stopped it occurring spontaneously, they can learn in this way to make a problem beat itself, and the buzz they get from success on a few occasions is often enough to turn off the anxiety and unblock the normal mechanism. If their self-estimate has been distorted as a cause or a result of their handicap, they may need more counseling, but at least whereas they were impotent, now they can ball. By a similar technique, women can get delightful control over their pelvic muscles.

As with analysis, how good a trip you get in consulting a behavior therapist depends on whom you consult: if he's uptight he'll try to make your behavior fashionable rather than rewarding. It's expensive, like all other help in America, but you get results in a few weeks, not 15 years, and the results are tangible. Unfortunately, the sexually reabled don't advertise like other patients, or it would be more widely known and used.

biofeedback

Doctors and yogis have long suspected that there are precious few body processes which can't to some extent be controlled by the mind. The trouble about controlling, say, one's blood pressure by taking thought is that one has no way of monitoring it. We have a full set of muscles to move our ears, but as we can't see the results of using these muscles it's difficult to learn specific movements. If, however, you watch your ears on closed-circuit television, which doesn't reverse like a mirror, you can learn to waggle them in a single session.

It's now known that blood pressure, skin blood flow, erection, and even brain electrical activity can be controlled voluntarily if you have a readout of what is happening and play hotter, colder with it. Fooling about with brain waves has become a West Coast party trick

(luckily it seems to be harmless, and even an aid to meditation), and the same device can be used to teach sufferers to turn off epileptic fits. Biofeedback-based control of sexual processes has a growing use in teaching women to co-ordinate their pelvic muscles, and impotent men to produce voluntary erection like a yogi. See *Behavior therapy*.

books
We're not knocking competitors, but the main thing here really is to avoid being badly misinformed. Sex books are mostly written by nonplaying coaches of limited experience, some of whom never saw an act of inter-course, or by sexually active and quite humane people who don't, however, know any human biology and get their medical information from old books. Both tend to be based on the psychiatry and sexology of 1874 not 1974. This doesn't of course apply to all books – modern field studies like those of Kinsey or Masters and Johnson, for example (though some of these are deliberately written in goon-language so that local policemen won't under-stand them: if they were interesting they might get banned – it doesn't do to let ordinary people read about sex). Magazines are getting franker about sexual behaviors, but contain a lot of fantasy and hogwash about rejuvena-tion remedies, potency pills, etc. The most realistic source of sexual comment is often the cartoons in *Playboy*, *Oui* and similar publications.

Moral and medical ax-grinders are fairly easy to spot. Beyond that, it's safe to say that any alarmist comment, or comment which suggests that something you both enjoy doing is immature, mentally unhealthy, etc., is likely to be bunk. The best test of a book is whether it's obvious the author really enjoys sex himself, and recog-nizes its infinite variety.

If you have straight questions or want book lists, try the Sex Information and Education Council of the US, 1855 Broadway, New York, NY, or the National Sex Forum, 330 Ellis, San Francisco.

doctors
We pointed out in *The Joy of Sex* that doctors aren't trained in sex counseling, or are only just beginning to be. On the other hand, they could do it well if they were, and in any case they're the first people to be consulted over sex problems.

You can get some idea of the quality of the advice a doctor gives you by noting his general demeanor. Re-assurance is a proper medicine, but be a little doubtful if you get hormone pills for impotence in the first instance, and very doubtful, to the point of consulting someone else, if you're told that it's your age, or nothing can be done and you should live with impotence, frigidity or premature ejaculation. With tricky problems doctors will refer you to a reputable sexologist, if there is one and the doctor is clued (referral to a teaching hospital is always a good move), to a gynecologist, a genito-urinary (g.u.) surgeon if you're male, or a psychiatrist. A gynecologist is obviously right if the trouble is pain, an anatomical thing, or subfertility. If it's the latter, don't go back to that clinic if they don't ask to see your husband too. You can save unnecessary investigations on yourself – he may have no sperms and will enjoy masturbating into a test tube more than you enjoy being insufflated, etc. The g.u. surgeon is a counsel of despair for all but anatomical male sex problems – some g.u. men are good on counseling the impotent or the over-quick; others aren't. The psychiatrist is often a cop-out – he may well be the best person if you have a problem such as depression (q.v.) or big emotional difficulties, but some doctors are liable to refer to him any behavioral problems that they can't handle themselves.

It is much better to insist on seeing a reputable sex counselor for any of the more common malfunctions – he'll call in the psychiatrist, the endocrinologist, the gynecologist, or whatever, if he thinks that they will be able to help you.

With reluctant counselors, change your doctor or be a nuisance until you get satisfaction. Don't let a major hangup become a way of life.

encounter groups

These have become an immensely popular West Coast sport. Basically, they're group psychotherapy sessions run by amateurs in a high atmosphere of expectation with self-chosen members. Professional training doesn't guarantee good reading of human communication, and some amateurs are intuitive therapists of a high order. Others aren't, or are working off problems of their own on the other group members – a psychiatric training at least makes the trained therapist aware of this possibility. The amateurs also tend to be optimists. Being amateurs they get everyone straight counseling has failed to help, and they don't screen their entrants. In consequence unless they're lucky they can collect really mentally ill people, expose them without skilled direction, and send them right round the bend. Accordingly, though encounter doesn't hurt, and can benefit, the mentally robust, regular psychotherapists spend a fair amount of time undoing the damage done to disturbed people by equally disturbed group-leaders.

The general effect is of the apocryphal small ad, "Teach

yourself brain surgery – all you need is a mirror and a saw." An aggressive leader can do real harm – his group usually turns into a wolf pack and reduces the least dominant and most disturbed member to tears instead of increasing their self-esteem. There are encounter pundits who are immensely proud of this technique. Others turn into mutual admiration societies around a guru who basks in the parental role and hasn't the skills to make constructive use of it, including turning it off when no longer needed. Such a leader doesn't really want his disciples to be able to do without him, and he creates a disabling addiction.

Methods and theories apparently don't matter, as a controlled study by Professor Yalom at Stanford has shown – the personality of the leader does. Many are badly disturbed themselves. The good ones try to teach their method to disciples, but as their results depend on the kind of people they personally are, the disciples get indifferent success.

If you want to learn awareness in a context of social interaction, it's better to do it either in social interaction where the atmosphere is less excited, or in group sessions with a therapist who has been properly trained as a moderator. Training doesn't make all therapists good, but you don't hire an amateur heart surgeon.

exercises

It would be perfectly easy to draw up a schedule of structured experiences which would take a couple through all of the things which sexuality can express – maleness/femaleness, weaker/stronger, muscle/skin, trust, assertion, helplessness, oneness, tension, relaxation and so on. The best exercise is to do this yourselves.

If you've played through the sexual resources in The Joy of Sex for pleasure, play them through again for pleasure but also with the conscious intention of improving your ability to read and speak the language implicit in them. This doesn't make sex either self-conscious or spoil its spontaneity, any more than it spoils Madame Bovary if you read it both as a masterpiece and to improve your French.

You can set up your own exercise plays based on the ordinary resources of sex plus what we've said in this book. Quite small changes when you are fully excited – like having intercourse with one or both of you blindfold, or the woman fantasizing that she's a man and trying to get inside maleness – can greatly deepen and alter the ordinary pleasure experience. Don't confine yourself to experiences which immediately turn you on. Try experiencing maleness if it doesn't specially attract you, or femaleness if you're self-consciously male. If you're

very aggressive, in the positive sense, and a little untrusting where you don't control, try experiencing complete helplessness; or, if you're very unassertive, complete control of your partner. Do these things in the play and coital situation so that the experience is reinforced by orgasm. At the same time maximize any potentials you have but don't use; a very muscular man who doesn't already fully use his muscularity in orgasm should work out with his partner ways of doing so, but also work on total relaxation.

Rather than telling you exactly how to do these things by a set of exercise situations (which people are bound to try correspondence-course fashion), the best way of making sexuality into a development experience – super-gourmet sex if you like – is to devise them yourselves using the materials and the knowhow we've quoted, and angling what you do to your particular needs. Handled like this the joy of sex can be assertion training, relaxation therapy, encounter and sex-identity reinforcement as necessary.

Some examples:

anal sex	anal sensation
	defiance value, taboo-breaking
	man may fantasy another male
	man can experience penetration (with a dildo or vibrator)
bathing, sex in water	total skin experience
	body is weightless, flying
	infantile and possibly prenatal reminiscences
blindfold intercourse, massage, etc.	anonymity of partner
	sex of partner hidden
	surprise effect (cannot predict partner's initiatives)
bondage	weaker/stronger experience
	helplessness/assertiveness/trust
	not being responsible
	partner's initiatives outside your control: you control partner
	erotization of struggle

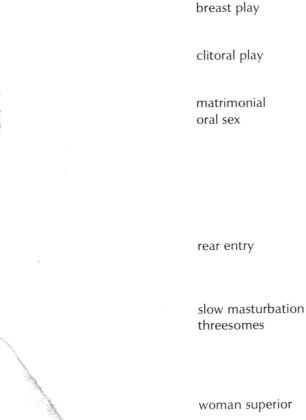

breast play	infancy flashback
	lover/child experience
	closeness, heart contact
clitoral play	sharpness of orgasm
	not being penetrated
	female fantasizes having a penis
matrimonial	relaxed oneness
oral sex	pleasure of sucking
	pheromones (odor hormone stimuli)
	intimacy, incorporating one another
	worthiness, cleanness of genitals
	going back to the womb
	taboo-breaking
rear entry	perineal stimulation
	back available for touch
	female invitation
	partner is anonymous
slow masturbation	total control of/by partner
threesomes	inviting a guest
	love-gift, non-jealousy
	dramatizing bisexuality
	relaxing male dominance (with a second male)
woman superior	better control for her
	trying-out sex roles
	he relinquishes responsibility
wrestling	muscular turnon
	weaker/stronger
	man stronger, dramatizes being taken
	woman stronger, dramatizes infancy reminiscence

meditation

Not at first sight an obvious resource for people with problems. It doesn't mean sitting and thinking about something, but rather achieving mentally a kind of zero-input condition. When this happens one becomes able to monitor internal brain traffic, to achieve altered states of mind, and – if one is a mystic and meditates systematically – "oceanic" states very similar to those induced in some people by LSD, but without its risks.

Peak experiences, if you happen to get them, do alter people beneficially, but the reason we include this as a counseling rather than a religious resource is that the meditative state, even at a very low level, has big effects on the autonomic nervous system and can relieve tension, while the more advanced experiences can help turn people off drugs or alcohol if they have the stamina to persist that far. You need an instructor to get started, and continuing instruction if you want to get further (otherwise some of the LSD-like effects can be scary for an unprepared person who isn't a natural meditative saint). Tantrics combined meditation with slow, non-orgasmic sex as an exercise in body-image manipulation, by which each one experienced himself or herself as simultaneously male and female. How far you go will depend on your religious talents – as a simple exercise in relaxation most people find meditation of quite a rudimentary kind rewarding.

psychoanalysis

A high proportion of prosperous Americans appear to visit the analyst weekly, as they visit the hairdresser – often with the expectation of getting help with personal or sexual problems. It is therefore worth looking at what analysis is, and what it isn't.

Freud's original technique of treating patients sprang from his discovery of infantile sexuality and repression. Adult sexual behaviors spring from extremely powerful emotions and responses existing in early infancy, in which the parents figure as sexual objects and the subject of desire, jealousy and so on, far ahead of any capacity for sexual performance. Repression is the programed putting out of mind by adults of a whole series of these infant experiences which nonetheless surface unbidden and influence behavior. Freud analyzed dreams, behaviors, attitudes and free-associations in order to make relevant parts of this infant experience conscious – explanation being used to enable the patient to experience (and hopefully come to terms with) those portions of this repressed background that were affecting his performance. Of all the subsequent psychoanalytic theorists who have modified these ideas, Freud still stands up best in the light of modern biological knowledge.

One key Freudian finding was that at one stage male toddlers experience intense anxiety about, and fear of losing, the genitalia, coupled with jealousy of the father – the so-called castration anxiety and Oedipus complex. We would now talk more about infantile sensuality instead of, or as well as, sexuality, and see the castration anxiety as a special case of a dominance situation. The penis is a dominance signal, and the mother's vulva is both an invitation and a threat – highly appropriate to a young prehuman male primate who had to stay with his mother, because he was immature, but avoid approaching her sexually because of the risk of being treated by the father as a competing adult male and vigorously attacked.

The reason that the penis is an obsession of Freudian interpretations is that it's an obsession of man. In most animals it takes adult plumage or voice to set off competition with other males, and one would expect beard anxiety rather than penis or castration anxiety. Man seems unique in picking a structure present from birth as a dominance signal – hairlessness, growing intelligence and upright posture may all have conspired to make a male recognizable, and hence competitive, while immature. What seems to have happened is that in evolution this whole package of behaviors has got moved to an irrelevantly early age.

Dominance anxiety *vis-à-vis* the father is, therefore, in all probability a temporary organ like the tadpole's tail, but it does profoundly affect adult behavior, as well as all human myth and literature. If avoidance of the female as your mother and a tabooed object is not satisfactorily reversed when the time comes to mate, a male may treat all women as a threat, and either prefer males, or need a transitional object (a fetish) in order to face them, as a child needs a teddy bear when anxious.

As to women, Freud postulated that they see themselves as already castrated and in search of the penis they have lost, while males are anxious to provide them with one in order to make them less threatening. Some of this sounds right and there's a fair amount of this thinking in folklore. Women do in some senses seek a penis, and men find phallicized women reassuring – witness the preference of some men for one-legged women, which is a simple schematic signal of the kind seen in animals. On the other hand, Freud himself didn't feel satisfied with his psychology of female sexuality, and we may well feel less so (we could do with a moratorium on theories about female sexuality devised by men). If you want a proper account of Freud's own ideas read his *Introductory Lectures on Psychoanalysis*, not what someone else says he said.

Both Freudian analysis and later variants (including that of Jung, who was interested in archetypes, or preferred patterns of human thinking, and in the male and female selves concealed in every individual) can be instructive and rewarding experiences and deepen self-comprehension. If they work, they are emotional or feeling experiences, not the equivalent of a lecture. In the course of self-comprehension some of our more irrational behaviors, such as being a perpetual loser, hating the other sex, or being accident-prone may be seen for what they are and relieved. For most concrete sexual problems, such as impotency, they're unfortunately far more instructive than beneficial. After ten years of analysis one may have garnered a lot of insight – and still be impotent or whatever other problem prompted you to seek help.

As an education analysis is well worth it if you can afford the time and the high cost. As a treatment for functionally autonomous habits that one is stuck with, whatever their infantile origins, the results are poor, and other kinds of attack are both quicker and more certain – scientifically operated relearning, for example (see *Behavior therapy*). At the same time many people who are cured of a symptom by behavior therapy could do with more insight (and can get it from nonclassical analytic methods like brief analysis and analytic group therapy, which are quicker and cheaper than Freud's original routine). Idiotic hostility occasionally reigns between analytic and behavioral practitioners, but they're both examining a programed learning process, and a primate biologist would knock their heads together.

All modern sexology and primatology has to take account of Freud. All discussion of human behaviors also has to take account of Jung, who was more sensitive to the realm of feelings but apt to take off into a kind of Wagnerian stratosphere, and of Adler, who was the first to point out (in other words) that a lot of what Freud classed as sexual anxieties in fact relate to dominance. These three weren't on speaking terms. It has taken primatology and anthropology to put them together into a general biology of human thinking and behavior – the way science gets delayed by dogma and ego-trips was a subject that none of them, unfortunately, tackled. Accordingly, the brand of analysis you get, if you have it, may depend on the school to which the analyst adheres, unless you get a sensible eclectic who knows all the theories. This matters less than you might think, because analysis is a sensitive experience in communication and intuition between you and the analyst, and it is this that imparts any benefit you may get from the sessions.

psychotherapy

Almost anything that makes you feel better mentally – from reassurance to ten years of analysis. It's mainly used of specific situations of dialogue or interaction which are designed to impart insight and overcome problems, and nearly all of it depends on the language of human non-verbal as well as verbal communication. Even going to the doctor with a pain somewhere can be a form of this (quite a lot of symptoms are messages or demonstrative behaviors) and a good doctor, beside giving you some aspirin for the pain, will read your body language and deal with the message through his own verbal and non-verbal communication to you.

Psychiatrists didn't invent what are called transference and counter-transference (the interaction of the patient's image of the doctor and the doctor's image of the patient – the doctor is a person, too): it's a normal form of human communication. More specific psychotherapy can involve letting someone talk (and make up his or her own mind over courses of action), while the therapist listens both to the verbal and the nonverbal information and responds helpfully. This can be a little like holding the mirror to enable someone to see into his own ears. Only you can get your head together, but a skilled outside observer can see things you don't, and enable you to see them.

Group psychotherapy saves time and maximizes the flow of this kind of information because there are several individuals of both sexes and a number of different make-ups interacting. A single therapist can only be of one sex at a time (so can't witness your reaction to the other sex) and starts with a built-in "parental" role. You came to him or her as an authority or a magician with the expectation of relief, and this doesn't expose, for example, your degree of dominance in a group. A really expert group therapist usually stays pretty quiet, reads the group interactions, and intervenes either to keep order (protecting anyone who gets picked on, asking an overtalkative member to give others a turn if the others don't ask him), or to guide the interaction so that members see for themselves what is occurring between them. It's a valuable experience to test yourself in such an environment even if you don't have gross problems.

You can learn even more about yourself through psychodrama in which members of the group act out their feelings to one another, or to figures like parents, spouses or employers. This can go on to straight social training: a shy person can learn to address a person of the opposite sex by playing a little charade, with the others giving comment and suggestions. An office door-mat can learn to deal with his boss and colleagues by letting other group members play them, and seeing where he is going wrong. This is rather the way in which some schools teach salesmen. One form of psychodrama is assertion training, which teaches you the skills and signals of higher dominance (without being overaggressive) when your self-esteem is low, using games and support from the group.

All psychotherapy aims to give you accurate information about yourself (insight), pinpoint hangups, and substitute more appropriate social skills. Its main use is in getting rid of general problems arising from your attitude and behaviors. It doesn't usually attack specifically sexual hangups directly, though problems like frigidity, if they're based on fears or mistaken beliefs about yourself and about sex, often improve, and so do physical symptoms which arise from things like constant anxiety or low self-esteem. The skills you learn from good group therapy make you a more fully interacting and signal-reading human being and better able to interpret your sex role *vis-à-vis* others. It is, however, a living and a learning process, not magic, and it won't undo a lot of bad learning experiences overnight.

sex therapy

Good sex therapists use – or know about – all of the techniques in this section, and fit horses to courses. At clinics treatment is of three main kinds: giving straight reassurance and information; giving specific treatment schedules for managing a particular problem (this is often really a form of behavior therapy); and couple-counseling. This is best done by the technique pioneered by Masters and Johnson, where a couple counsels a couple, so nobody is in a minority of one. All sex therapy involves seeing both partners and going into their attitudes, fears and expectations – not just into the presenting problem.

Quite a lot of couples come not because someone is impotent, frigid or otherwise in trouble but because they want to improve their sexual relationship in depth. Accordingly, one excellent kind of background therapy, specific problems or not, is for the counselor to put together a group of couples and let them talk, in the course of which they find that all of their problems are shared. For more detailed overcoming of a specific difficulty, the best practical helper is your normal partner (if not, you've got the wrong partner). The therapists talk through attitudes, get rid of nonsenses, and brief the couple on the best way of giving themselves the requisite behavior therapy. Showing videotapes or films of a really relaxed couple can help others who are uptight or lack knowhow.

Good sex counseling is badly needed, and doctors unfortunately are not trained to give it. The problem in finding the right person to consult is that freaks and

quacks aren't uncommon. If you want an address in your area, try calling the Sex Information and Education Council of the US. When you go to a clinic you will not forthwith be handed over for instruction to a surrogate partner: you should both be interviewed, together and separately (distrust a therapist who doesn't suggest this) and you should get an estimate of the expected cost and duration of treatment. Some church bodies support sex therapy clinics which are open-minded and not committed to religious dogmas of behavior. Any therapist who suggests sleeping with one or both of you is a phoney: that isn't the therapist's role.

If you can't afford help or get it in any other way, you could well try to convene a group of couples in your area, by way of a small ad or otherwise, and try to get them talking. This in itself is therapy, and people help each other, even if they don't know the answers. You could then try to get someone who does know some answers in to assist. Try to include one knowledgeable, uninhibited and sexually alert pair, both to get the others talking and to put down common misconceptions – that oral sex is abnormal, for example, or that impotence is a physical disease. This is a second best but better than nothing, and the group can supplement their experience by reading. We don't want to sound like a commercial, but this book and *The Joy of Sex* could be used in this way. Unlike most other matter written about sex they represent modern knowledge, not obsolete folklore, at least as far as the range of normal behaviors is concerned.

And don't be deterred from seeking help if the idea of any kind of group discussion offends you. Good therapists work in complete privacy, and won't suggest talking to others or taking part in group discussion unless you both wish it and think it would help you.

We've talked here about therapy with couples. If you have no partner, have a problem, and need help with it, you can be helped by other techniques, so don't be deterred from seeking advice.

surrogates

The best way to learn to have sex if you're new to it or have problems is to have it with a clued, experienced, undemanding and turned-on partner. Unfortunately, most of our regular partners are also learning, don't as a rule have all that much experience and have hangups. They are also involved in the bind over "Am I pleasing him/her?" "Why isn't he/she pleasing me?" which gets worse the more the other party has performance troubles. Hookers are clued, experienced and sometimes turned on, but the scene is wrong, and a lot of them, by motivation and by experience, are basically hostile to the opposite sex – also, unless you go to very expensive call girls, their time is money and they time-stress you.

When someone consults a sex therapist over a problem such as premature ejaculation, if he has a partner the therapist will instruct the couple. How about a male who has gay experience only and wants to acquire heterosexual skills? Holy society used to tell him to get married (which could be heavy for the wife if he has made the wrong decision in trying), less holy used to suggest prostitutes or pickups, risking a lot of mischief if a failure led to a putdown. Unless you think sex can be taught by correspondence course, a sane therapist would send him to a woman with the necessary skills, who enjoys sex and is supportive but doesn't make demands. (We say "he" and "woman" because that's the way around it is now: there are male surrogates, but from a cultural backlog women are very often less able to accept them

than men are female surrogates, and there are psycho-dynamic differences. We don't know enough male sur-rogates to be able to judge how this will go.)

The woman who is a surrogate has to enjoy sex, be clued about handling male problems, and be warm and caring, but tough enough not to get overinvolved with clients. She always works with the therapist who referred the patient to her, and takes responsibility for the line of treatment. Surrogate and client are introduced – first names if they prefer – and spend the first few sessions getting used to being naked together. He may never have had the chance to explore a woman's body. Her job is to reinforce him without scaring him, to cultivate his potency, to teach him social as well as sexual skills in bed, and to concentrate on his presenting problem (premature ejaculation is perhaps the one surrogates most often tackle). Quite as much as training in performance he gets training in unhurried relaxation, and catches her confident, undemanding attitude toward sex.

So far from being an exploitation of women, some surrogates find their job an ideal expression of their own needs, though it's hard work, like any other wet-shoulder assignment. They and their clients don't become mutually dependent or fall madly in love, but stay close friends. One surrogate we know wept with pleasure, not jealousy, at getting a letter to say that an ex-client was happily married and owed it all to her. It's a warm, rewarding human relationship, given the right people, with nothing clinical or prossy about it.

Sensible doctors have used surrogates for years but kept quiet about it. Now they can do so openly, which is much to the good.

Special
Needs

alcohol

Alcohol is one of the common causes of impotence: people forget that it's a powerful sedative.

What commonly happens is that a male has an off night – they come home from a party, and he finds he can't get it up. She may or may not say something which hits his ego, but he spends next day getting up steam to show her (or himself), has several drinks to fortify himself, then tries the virility bit – meaning straight-in intercourse with no relaxation, no preliminary touching, and no help from her. This is failure number two. With luck he will wake with an erection, but we've known males who failed to use this, insisting that they must produce one when they wanted. This kind of self-frustration can rapidly build into habitual impotence, with an equally habitual two or three martinis an evening guaranteeing that failure will continue.

Most Americans simply don't realize how much they do drink. It can easily run to half a bottle of spirit, in one form or another, per day, and this is enough to cut male response quite heavily, in spite of the status of sub-intoxication as a virility symbol. Most males survive this, but many more would be multiorgasmic if they cut down on the ingestion of a sexual blunting agent. Moreover, since premature ejaculation is a form of nascent impotence, drink doesn't help that either – it's more liable to turn it into the complete variety.

Alcoholism, in an alcohol culture, is difficult to recognize. Basically anyone whose behavior is altered by drinking in a way deleterious to himself or others is an alcoholic. Alternatively imagine that it were announced that as from tomorrow the world supply of alcoholic drinks had dried up: a normal reaction might be "damn!" – an alcoholic's reaction would be "how do I get through the day after tomorrow?"

Alcoholism is a disease, not a weakness of character or a fault. It's quite one of the most disruptive things which can affect a couple's relationship because of the long stretches of non-communication, the unreality of the drunken party's behavior, and the character changes that go with it. It's useless to pose a choice between drink and you, because drink will be chosen. There is no alternative to treatment, either through community psychotherapy with Alcoholics Anonymous, or by other methods such as behavior therapy (q.v.). The main problem is to get it recognized early by the sufferer – at the stage when the other partner starts a game of hide and seek to avoid drinking occasions or liquor in the house, and the sufferer starts playing to circumvent these efforts. Often nothing is said during this game, but it's diagnostic and the time for plain speaking if serious problems are to be avoided.

depression

Depression is probably the commonest cause of sudden loss of sexual feeling in people who have so far been functioning well.

In severe depression, which can come on gradually or suddenly, there is a loss of all satisfaction in life. Surroundings appear drab or tasteless, there may be a sensation of cut-offness, tiredness is intense, and is accompanied by feelings of despair, misery, guilt and so on which can lead to suicide. This is a medical emergency. Some people have recurrent attacks, others one only. It can follow normal grief at a bereavement or a putdown, but is quite different in feel. Depression of this kind is a biochemical illness affecting brain amines. It doesn't respond well to psychotherapy, but can almost always be relieved by drugs. These take about two weeks to act, and it may be necessary to try more than one kind of drug before finding one appropriate to a given person. Recurrent attacks can be prevented by the mineral lithium, but this must be taken continuously and the blood levels monitored by a laboratory. Some of the drugs used to treat depression can turn off sexual performance, increasing anxiety and despair if they do, but this is a side effect and soon passes off.

Severe depression often but not always leads to loss of libido, as it leads to loss of appetite generally. It is also usually obvious that the person is ill – to others, if not to them. The depressions which present sex problems are mild depressions; the patient doesn't feel depressed so much as ill (without symptoms), tired and turned off. They may suddenly become frigid or impotent, and that doesn't help. A lot of the trouble in treating them is in persuading them that they are depressed, not just glum and unlucky, and it's only when medication lifts the mood that they realize how depressed they were. Untreated mild depression can drag on for years. If you suspect it in yourself or your partner, get it treated.

A lot of counseling and psychotherapy have been wasted on these mild, long-lasting changes in brain chemistry. The treatment is the same as for the severer kinds and is within the competence of any doctor. The trouble is that some psychiatrists are apt to turn on the entire talk show when what is needed is one of the types of drug which restore the normal chemistry in your head. You may indeed need counseling as well, but that should accompany or follow medical treatment of the main illness. Always suspect depression if you or your partner cease without any good reason to function or to enjoy. Depressions get better in the end, and any therapy you have had over the years gets the credit. Modern tricyclic or MAOI drugs do the job in between two weeks and two months.

disablement

Disabled people – even severely disabled people – can use both this book and *The Joy of Sex*. At first sight, since we obviously describe a lot of things one can't do if badly paralyzed or otherwise handicapped, they might look depressing to anyone with these problems. But in fact, because they cover the whole range of sex behaviors, not simply straight intercourse, you will realize, if you think about it, that you can use them as a dyspeptic or a diabetic can use a cookbook.

Minor disability may only limit your choice of positions, etc. Major disability will mean that you may have to carve out a whole special form of sex for yourself. Virtually nobody is too disabled to have some pleasure from sexuality – with a partner if you can, without one if you must. Generations of disabled people have been hocused out of this by other people's embarrassment, the pattern of institutions, and the desire of society to suppress any sexual expression which was suppressible. Everyone needs tenderness and contact, but it needn't stop there. If you are immobile, or if you have difficulty using your genitalia in the usual way, you can still beat the handicap, by using non-genital sensation, by finding out what resources you have got. Your biggest problem, after that of getting well people to treat you as a person, will be in getting it through their heads that you have the same needs as they have. How to do this is a constant topic of conversation where badly handicapped people get together (usually not in front of the hospital staff, who pretend as often as not that "we don't have those problems here").

Gradually, however, things are getting better, and counseling help is being made available if you insist (don't settle for Pollyanna or talk about coming to terms with reality if that means accepting that a physical disability means you have to be an involuntary monk or nun and like it). Your first big problem isn't the disability but other people's hangups – most nurses won't help two disabled folk to get into position for lovemaking, and few institutions provide privacy, even if they recognize the need, even for masturbation. But given determination you can beat this. We know one badly handicapped couple who have a really tender sex life, even though they only have the hospital bathroom – she uses her mouth and he his big toe.

If your disability goes back a long way you have a lot of fears and worries to live down; if it's recent, like a wound or an accident, you've got the shock of picking up the pieces. It's easier if one partner isn't disabled, and if you've already had a sex life; you'll have to reprogram it in terms of what you still have. Paraplegics can often make love and enjoy it – males can usually get an erection even if they can't feel below the waist, and extragenital sensation grows with practice in both sexes. We can't counsel here in detail, but at least we've described many ways of getting sexual pleasure, some of which almost any disabled person can manage. The big thing is to resist the pressures to become an unsexual unperson.

Above all, get rid of the idea that nobody can love, or have pleasure with, a disabled person. It simply isn't true. Thousands can and do. In fact, the need to give special help to people with impaired mobility, etc., may be the beginning of a general move in medicine to give proper sexual help to everyone who needs it. It has been the need of these people which has brought home to doctors that at the moment there is little or no proper sex counseling at a practical level for anyone. In your case, couples with the same kind of disability as you who have fought their way through could probably help most, plus a change in the attitude of institution and nursing staff. In the last resort you can only get this by fighting.

How far sexual prostheses can help disabled people is a matter for research: cultivation of skin, breast and other sensation and straightforward couple ingenuity are a better bid. We think that swinging couples with good experience could help more than psychiatrists or doctors here, and we wish there was an organization through which they could give this sort of help – there must be many who would be willing and glad to do so.

disablement practicalities

Preaching is unproductive, and it is difficult, beyond what we've said, to help with the emotional side of disablement simply through books. With the physical side and at the purely mechanical level one can do a lot more. Often the first disability to be overcome, especially in males, is one which affects plenty of robust and un-injured people – the idea that sex is about the genitalia, and that sexualizing any other part of the body is perverse. We have to take it that you know that this is hogwash, and that you are ready to use your skin, hands, feet, mouth and whatever, and so is your partner.

That accepted, start with an analysis of what, in the normal range of sex, you can't do. For minor disabilities one often finds that the whole problem arises from fanatical adherence to the missionary position. A woman with an arthritic hip who can't bend or open her legs can often be taken from behind, with a lot of clitoral and breast play to help arousal. A man with a bad back can let the woman come astride. Some disabilities, in one or both partners, may mean you can't use the penis at all – if so, go for hand, mouth and skin work (but if the man can get any erection, don't assume intercourse is impossible until you've thought of, and tried, all the possible forms of apposition). One group with special problems are the paraplegic, who have impaired or absent sensation and little voluntary movement below the waist. Nearly all paraplegic males can get erections and ejaculate but can't feel what is happening, but they can and do enjoy intercourse, especially with a partner who can evoke skin sensitivity in the upper parts of the body. Women, especially if they have been sexually experienced before they were injured, can often get a full orgasm from breast play, and intermammary intercourse can give them still better participation. With severer disabilities the scope can be still further reduced. But if you have any sensation in your clitoris, penis, breasts or mouth, you can experience sexual arousal, and if you can move your tongue, fingers or big toe you can do something to arouse a partner.

For everyone, disabled or not, partner arousal and climax is at least half of the reward of sex. Set about outwitting the problem by fantasizing a kind of sexual play either within, or better, just outside, your capacity for physical movement, and then see if you and your partner can bring it about. Allow for quite a few failures. If you *can* in privacy make a game of it, do so (hard as it may be to take this advice from an undisabled counselor. If it helps, the author of this piece lost most of a hand in boyhood. The surviving thumb is a marvelous and reliable sexual implement). Make full use of fantasy, pornography and the like if they turn you on. With a widespread special problem like multiple sclerosis or paraplegia, contact your national organization or talk to other couples with the same problem. Best of all, try to get a group together who can break down reticence over all this and share their experiences – with a sex counselor on hand if you can find a good one. The National Sex Forum in San Francisco are already doing this. For some very disabled people, 69 gives a greater feeling of mutuality than intercourse, for others really creative mutual masturbation. For yet others, a combination of these with full or partial insertion becomes a pattern rewarding to both partners.

This assumes, of course, that you have a partner. For the lonely or the institutional disabled – some of them incapable of masturbating, a particularly cruel defect, or even watched by moralistic idiots to see they don't attempt it for lack of privacy – hope has to lie with society. In some Scandinavian institutions the caring administration of orgasm is the responsibility of the physiotherapist – certainly to our knowledge for males, and, one must hope, for everyone, despite the sick idea that women don't need it or would find it immodest. Is anyone going to oppose this openly? Probably not, but they'd oppose it secretly, arguing that the patients would be embarrassed, the therapists would leave and all the usual repertoire of reasons. But progress can be made. When one patient openly demanded privacy to masturbate, nobody spoke up at once in support, the authorities blushed, and arranged it unobtrusively for everyone. It can be done, while society learns the abc of concern for sexual realities. Undisabled people could take a hand too – it would be a bigger sign of caring than taking round library books. In our view, nobody need feel embarrassed either to give or to receive.

heart attacks

There are two points here – avoiding them and coping with them sexually.

All exercise protects to some extent against heart attacks provided it isn't too violent and intermittent in sedentary people. Sex is good exercise but is intermittent, so you need walking as a backup. There's no numerical evidence that it favors longevity to be sexually active, though one would expect it, and there's plenty of anecdotal evidence, not it's true that horny people live long, but that long-lived people are unusually horny. In the present state of the art, it looks as if the main causes of the epidemic of coronaries in males are cigarette smoking, tension and the excessive consumption of animal fats. On the evidence, cigarettes are probably the top hazard (the fact that it is possible that heavy smokers are constitutionally tense doesn't explain away the incidence figures), dairy products the second, and obesity and tension the third. No sane person would now eat butter, cream, bacon or saturated fats generally – the answer to the question why our peasant forebears ate them with impunity is probably that they took vast amounts of exercise and didn't usually live into the coronary age.

If you have a heart attack, you need to get gentle sex started again as soon as you can start gentle exercise. Heart attacks don't affect potency but, apart from anything else, are commonly followed by depression (q.v.), partly because they're frightening and depressing and partly for physical reasons, and a return to sex combats this. There's not much risk in a wife giving even a recumbent man an orgasm in bed (heart attacks in women are much rarer, so it's usually this way round), and early intercourse can be lateral, or with her astride, or by gentle but fairly rapid masturbation or mouth work. You can judge whether medical advice is being overcautious or not from what you know of the doctor. If he says "no sex" ask why – sex is an important part of rehabilitation, and a clued cardiologist will only advise waiting if he has a reason.

Relaxed sex, even if it's violent, only rarely provokes a heart attack – very anxious sex scenes more often do. Either is far less hazardous than gardening, or even having a severe nightmare, which seems to account for some nocturnal attacks.

later life

In *The Joy of Sex* we explained that sexuality doesn't run out with age, that given good health and an expectation of carrying on, potency doesn't decline, but that male response changes.

In organizing your sex life from about 60 on, the things to remember are these:

1   Men normally attain fewer orgasms but no fewer erections as they get older. If their normal frequency of intercourse is high, they may get one orgasm in three to five instead of every time. They can get an orgasm every time if the couple switch techniques after she has come, and change to oral or manual stimulation; though if you use hard rubbing, the orgasm rate in coitus may fall further, through desensitization. Don't cut your rate of intercourse below what you've been used to, because with age sexual response, like muscular strength, is very susceptible to disuse, and never drop it altogether or you may have trouble restarting. In partnerless periods, use regular masturbation, but don't hurry it: practice holding a full erection each time. The fall in orgasm frequency means that you must reprogram in the expectation of not coming every time, and concentrate on your partner's feelings.

2   Spontaneous erections also get fewer. All normal males over about 55 need some direct tactile stimulus to the penis on many or most occasions. A lot of older males who say they often can't get it up are waiting for divine inspiration when what they need is hand work. Get it up yourself – better still, your partner should do it.

3   Women's sexual feelings only decline after the menopause if they are upset about it or think that they should decline. However, over the menopause itself hormone changes plus psychic factors can produce libido swings, and a longish time after there may be vaginal dryness. Regular sex seems to keep hormonal balance going, but many women now get proper substitution therapy. This is cosmetically good, preserves their feeling of well-being if that was impaired, and avoids the loss of bone minerals which leads to the little old lady condition in the 70s and 80s with shrinkage of the skeleton. The only snag about this, with a couple who are both in later life, is that hormone therapy often makes the vagina a lot wetter than it was premenopausally, and the man, used to a fair degree of friction, may suddenly find he

gets virtually no feeling from insertion. This calls for a change in the prescription, but it's worth mentioning because males who've been scared by propaganda about aging often think they're going impotent.

4 A regular partner who ages only gets ugly and undesirable to a loving man if she really lets herself go. Familiarity and experience more than make up for magazine looks, and older men who've had both find young girls' lack of knowhow offputting. On the other hand, men do get turned off, and can become impotent, as a result of disfiguring obesity, slobbishness or sudden adoption of a senile style of makeup. Good and responsible plastic surgery (to immense pendulous udder-like breasts, for example) can help here if the problem is gross, but don't be talked into expensive face-lifting maneuvers unless you really trust the surgeon. This is a very bad area for con-men, and you can get robbed and disfigured as well as disappointed. If you need plastic surgery, consult a university medical school, not a clinic operator.

Ultimately, and especially with ill-health, your frequency of intercourse will go down, but it will never pinch out until you do, and you may find yourself developing the skills of touching, hand work and so on which you learned but didn't use so much when you were more coitally active. All you are doing is shifting your repertoire to meet a less vigorous style of lovemaking. Fifteen per cent of married people over 78 in a recent study were having regular intercourse, and that makes no allowance for couples where one partner was sick, or where they'd never had much of a sex life anyway. In fact, since highly active people sexually remain highly active (either because they were sexy to start with, or because practice improves function, or both), that 15 per cent was probably made up of couples who had really developed their sexuality earlier. Violently muscular and fantasy-based sex play probably does decline, but new modes take its place if you are versatile.

Where the couple is of unequal age the man is usually the older. If there's a big difference in age, the wife needs to be clued about the normal changes in male response. If for any reason her preferred orgasm frequency is higher than his at this stage, she shouldn't push it, but they should talk, and cultivate nonerectile extras to make up the trade gap: similarly in the reverse situation – though a woman who doesn't feel every time isn't as vulnerable as a man who is trying to outdo his erectile physiology.

masochism

A masochist, contrary to folklore, isn't necessarily a person who likes being beaten, jumped on by people in boots, and the like. Krafft-Ebing borrowed the name of a

Viennese novelist with these and other fantasies to make a self-adhesive label for a big range of behaviors, most of which, when dramatized sexually, are unimportant. The beatees and jumpees may be acting out all or part of a spectrum which involves straight skin and muscle exploration, trying out various roles for size, and real masochism, which is the desire to be punished in expiation of sexuality (and even, with some dedicated masochists, in expiation of existing at all).

Society has succeeded in laying a little of this feeling on most of us, but when it links up with other infantile mislearning about the body image, or with psychosis, it can be heavy. Real masochists may prefer sexual plays associated symbolically with pain, low self-esteem, worry over sex roles and punishment, but, far more important, in daily life they are defeatist and accident-prone. This can be bewilderingly consistent, in that they manage somehow to be involved in misfortunes that couldn't have been organized, like being robbed or mugged. Accident-proneness is in their body language and attracts lightning.

People like this make dangerous partners not because the same pattern of fantasy appears in their sexual play, but because of their capacity to arrange their own and other people's unhappiness, and the way they seduce partners into noncommunicating exploitation. Accordingly, don't bother about preferences for rough or submissive sexual play – these often fulfill other quite normal exploratory needs and act as a lightning-conductor for traces of guilt in healthy people. Look out rather for the person who is a wholetime willing dog's-body overtaken by an unreasonable number of Job-like misfortunes – accidents, car crashes, getting gypped, bankruptcies, you name it. Being emotionally kicked around by one or by a succession of exploitative partners is more important as an index than the character of directly sexual fantasy, though this, as with everyone, will match the person.

Being guilty at a deep level over sex and body feeling is a grave disability, sexually and socially. It leads to an inability to express any kind of aggression (q.v.) except against oneself, and often ends in a fatal accident or in actual suicide. If you notice the traits we've listed in yourself or a partner, get help. This is an instance where psychoanalysis (q.v.) or some briefer form of psychotherapy (q.v.) is probably the best resource.

"Feminine masochism" (the idea that women are naturally masochistic) is a nonsense based on a misreading of the ethologically submissive behaviors – being penetrated, dramatizing helplessness and so on – by which female animals, including humans, turn on the male, turn off his hostility, and overcome (in humans) infantile anxieties about the dangerousness of women.

Liking him to take you, mini-rape style, isn't masochism – only the use of good mammalian equipment. Liking him to exploit or humiliate you socially is. With the social pressures withdrawn, modern women are only masochistic if they're really suffering from a deep-seated disorder of normal self-esteem.

The name masochism has outlived its use and should be returned to its owner. At the moment it's chiefly used to cause alarm and despondency over normal play behaviors. For the actual disorder, we prefer simply low dominance.

We have talked about masochists, not sadists, because normal people won't maintain a couple relationship with a person who, for reasons exactly like those which make the masochist a loser, tries to act out a dominance he or she doesn't have by hurting or humiliating others. If such a situation persists, the persisting half is a masochist. Sadists can and do hurt people sexually, not so much by violence, though this can happen, as by humiliating or rejecting loving people who don't recognize their abnormality. But the violent or subpsychotic kind are a real hazard of sex play with strangers, particularly symbolically aggressive sex play, which may stop being play and turn to earnest. Child play can do the same if there are no adults around to control it. Any situation in which one person plays at dominating another as a sexual game is safe only on a basis of perfect trust, or in the presence of sane people who can see it stays playful. Anything else is dangerous.

overweight

Overweight can be genetic (there are fat families); it can be due to a disorder of the body image which leads to overeating; or it can be due, quite simply, to gluttony. In our culture gross overeating is a norm. Anyone who lived on full restaurant portions would be overweight.

Fatness due to too much food shortens life in both sexes and can interfere considerably with potency in the male. The only way to lose weight is to eat less. No gimmicks work. Either you do it voluntarily, with some community support from bodies like Weight Watchers, or you get a diet (from a doctor, not a cranky paperback) and adhere to it, or you are put on appetite-reducing drugs. Commercial ripoffs usually act by making you lose water. There is no way, advertisements notwithstanding, of losing weight locally. Gross cases can have an intestinal bypass operation, but this is an emergency measure. For healthy women, having the fat scraped off by a cosmetic surgeon is an example of unnecessary surgery in search of a fool to exploit. It can disfigure you for life, and often does. Don't fall into the opposite error, if you're female, and be hocused by fashion into adopting the Belsen line – it's no more sexy than a family of chins. Women normally have subcutaneous fat and are cello-shaped – don't tempt the Almighty. Most cultures appreciate normal curves, and ours will if you resist sales talk.

Fat people often need to develop their own sexual techniques: for the man, intercourse with someone who is moderately overweight is pleasanter than with someone underweight. If approach is tricky, she can lie face up over the edge of the bed and he can stand or kneel. It's often worth developing rear approaches making full use of her buttocks. If he has a belly, she will need to be at right-angles to him, either on their sides with her leaning back or astride, or with him over the bed edge and her standing astride – he won't be able to come on top, and will quite often prefer to avoid male-active positions because of breathlessness. As with disablement (q.v.) play this as a game and try to find your own best-fit positions. Meanwhile do something about the overweight, in the interests both of sex and of general health. It's ridiculous and dangerous to carry a permanent 50 lb girdle.

pregnancy

The normal human pattern is to go on having sex all through pregnancy, and the pregnant woman is more, not less, attractive to many males, increased tenderness and closeness apart. You may need to switch to different postures (and avoid very deep or violent ones) when she gets really big. Some women get markedly decreased desire during pregnancy – in most it tends to swing more than usual, both for hormonal and psychic reasons. If she gets morning sickness she'll need gentleness first thing on waking.

If you miscarry easily it may be wise to avoid not only orgasm but even intercourse around the twelfth week and in the last two months. Take medical advice on this if it's your problem, but distrust total offhand prohibitions, and at least discuss them. You need sex at this time for closeness.

Pregnancy can have quite odd psychological effects on the male, from the immature guy who feels left out and goes on the tiles when his wife is in labor, to the man who stakes his share in the process by getting toothache or stomach cramps – or even a dummy pregnancy by swallowing air. Don't be surprised if you feel this way – it's a common human behavior, ritualized by some cultures, who put the father as well as the mother to bed for delivery (the *couvade*). Its function is to include the father and not make him feel guilty that she has the labor while he has the fun.

Quite the best pregnancy position for intercourse is on your sides from behind, though both of you may need intelligent handwork as well. In other positions the man will have to control depth; she can help by putting her hand round the penis root. Use the occasion to cultivate the shallow techniques – they are worth it for their own sake. After delivery, you can usually restart as soon as healing is complete and discharge has stopped.

prostate

The prostate gland enlarges with age in many males. If it comes to obstruct the passage of urine, it may require surgery. This usually happens in the 60s and 70s. The vital thing is to have a full discussion with the surgeon before consenting to the operation, and avoid like the plague any surgeon who doesn't realize that 60- and 70-year-old people are still sexually active. Some kinds of prostatic surgery can interfere with potency, and it's up to you to insist that your potency be conserved, and the mode of operation planned with this in mind. If you do insist, you'll probably be able to enlist full co-operation, unless there is some absolute surgical indication for the riskier type of operation. Older men used routinely to be made impotent by younger men who think the old don't or shouldn't ball at their age. Sex itself doesn't hurt the prostate, though constant frustrated sexual arousal without orgasm possibly may.

Cancer of the prostate has to be treated by surgery, as a rule, and/or hormones, and the hormones given are apt to turn off potency quite apart from surgical damage. Discuss the options with the surgeon, and insist that the discussion be a full and a two-sided one.

vaginismus

The outward and visible sign of inner and spiritual uptightness – it's a condition in which a woman's muscles go into such intense spasm that she can't be penetrated at all. Often she is married and wants to be penetrated, but the reaction, like ticklishness, is beyond voluntary control. This condition explains the quite common cases in which a couple in love, with the male fully potent, have ended by giving up all attempts at penetration and either dropped sex or settled for half measures.

Don't settle for these, or let them get to be a habit, but shout for help early. The first step is to get the rest of her sensual and relaxed, and in this many of the forms of submedical body-awareness can help. The second is to tackle the spasm. This can be done by a behavioral therapist, or she can do it herself by buying a set of glass dilators, covering them with K-Y jelly, and learning to insert them, starting with one of little-finger size. She should do this lying over a bed edge in a warm room, alone (it's better if he doesn't help) and combining the process with learning to give herself good feelings manually (see *Masturbation and learning*). When she has got up to one rather bigger than a penis, let him try to insert it, with her eyes first open, then closed or covered, then some other object, such as a vibrator, and then his penis. A couple can do this themselves, or they may feel (especially if she's very nervous or it's gone on a long time) that they'd rather have skilled help from the start. Behavior therapy (q.v.) nearly always works if do-it-yourself desensitization doesn't.

Women with vaginismus aren't all basically unwilling to have sex, even at an infant level. In some there's a clear history of things being forced into the anus in childhood to cure constipation – soapsticks and the like. Luckily people don't do this any more, since it evidently can derange adult function quite badly.

Index